THE LEGEND OF

WORTHINGTON

INDUSTRIES

SECOND EDITION

THE LEGEND OF
WORTHINGTON
INDUSTRIES

Jeffrey L. Rodengen

Edited by Jon VanZile
Design and layout by Jill Apolinario & Dennis Shockley

For Bill and Judy Fisk, whose friendship,
like steel itself, is ever strong and
has taken so many wonderful shapes.

WRITE STUFF

Write Stuff Enterprises, Inc.
1001 South Andrews Avenue
Second Floor
Fort Lauderdale, FL 33316
1-800-900-Book (1-800-900-2665)
(954) 462-6657
www.writestuffbooks.com

Publisher's Cataloging in Publication

Rodengen, Jeffrey L.
    The legend of Worthington Industries, Inc./
Jeffrey L. Rodengen. – 2nd ed.
    p. cm.
    Includes bibliographical references and index.
    ISBN 0-945903-55-3

    1. Worthington Industries – History. 2. Steel industry and trade – United States – History.
I. Title

HD9519.W64R64 1999
338.7/669142/0973   QBI99-1363

Library of Congress
Catalog Card Number 99-071038

ISBN 0-945903-55-3

Completely produced in the
United States of America
10 9 8 7 6 5 4 3 2 1

Also by Jeffrey L. Rodengen

The Legend of Chris-Craft

*IRON FIST: The Lives
of Carl Kiekhaefer*

*Evinrude-Johnson and
The Legend of OMC*

*Serving the Silent Service:
The Legend of Electric Boat*

*The Legend of
Dr Pepper/Seven-Up*

The Legend of Honeywell

The Legend of Briggs & Stratton

The Legend of Ingersoll-Rand

*The Legend of Stanley:
150 Years of The Stanley Works*

The MicroAge Way

The Legend of Halliburton

*The Legend of
York International*

*The Legend of
Nucor Corporation*

*The Legend of Goodyear:
The First 100 Years*

The Legend of AMP

The Legend of Cessna

The Legend of VF Corporation

The Spirit of AMD

The Legend of Rowan

*New Horizons:
The Story of Ashland Inc.*

*The History of
American Standard*

The Legend of Mercury Marine

The Legend of Federal-Mogul

*Against the Odds:
Inter-Tel—The First 30 Years*

The Legend of Pfizer

*State of the Heart:
The Practical Guide to
Your Heart and Heart Surgery*
with Larry W. Stephenson, M.D.

*The Legend of
Trinity Industries, Inc.*

The Legend of IBP, Inc.

*The Legend of
Cornelius Vanderbilt Whitney*

The Legend of Amdahl

The Legend of Litton Industries

The Legend of Gulfstream

The Legend of Bertram
with David A. Patten

*The Legend of
Ritchie Bros. Auctioneers*

The Legend of ALLTEL
with David A. Patten

*The Yes, you can of
Invacare Corporation*
with Anthony L. Wall

*The Ship in the Balloon:
The Story of Boston Scientific
and the Development of
Less-Invasive Medicine*

The Legend of Noble Drilling

*Fifty Years of Innovations:
Kulicke & Soffa*

*Biomet–From Warsaw
to the World*
with Richard F. Hubbard

The Legend of Discount Tire Co.
with Richard F. Hubbard

The Legend of La-Z-Boy
with Richard F. Hubbard

TABLE OF CONTENTS

INTRODUCTION

WORTHINGTON INDUSTRIES is not exactly a household name. It does not beckon us along the highway when we travel, nor provide a quick lunch when we're on the run. We don't see Worthington on the air conditioners that keep us cool, the microwaves that heat our food or the batteries that run our children's toys — although the company has had a hand in making them. Worthington Industries does not produce or package a single product we use in the course of a day. Yet, for most Americans, the company is part of our daily lives.

Worthington Industries was born in 1955 in the basement of an apartment in Columbus, Ohio. In those days, five employees worked a lone piece of equipment under the direction of John H. McConnell. McConnell, a former steel worker who had attended college on the GI Bill, believed that a niche was developing in the steel industry as the major producers built larger mills and moved away from smaller tonnage and specialized orders. McConnell borrowed $600 against his car and set about to fill that void.

Over the next few years, The Worthington Steel Company created the value-added steel processing industry, in which steel is processed to the exact gauge, width, length, surface finish and temper specified by customers in a variety of industries, including automotive, appliance, electrical, communication, office equipment, machinery and leisure.

In 1968, the company made its first public stock offering. One year later, investors were treated to a 26.8 percent increase in sales, which topped $21 million.

Since then, the company's record has been astonishing. In all but three years of its history as a public company, Worthington has posted record sales and earnings, establishing an average annual growth rate in earnings per share of 22 percent over its first 40 years. A $750 investment in 1968, with dividends reinvested, would have earned more than $265,000 in just 27 years.

In 1971 Worthington Steel changed its name to Worthington Industries to reflect its expansion into new areas of business. That year, the company purchased a small, unprofitable cylinder manufacturer and turned it into the leading producer of steel and aluminum pressure cylinders in the United States. Over the next 25 years, Worthington continued to expand its steel processing and cylinder manufacturing capabilities through strategic acquisitions in the South and Northeast, and through increasingly innovative technologies.

By 1990, the company that began with a single slitter was able to perform all levels of value-added steel processing services, such as pickling, blanking, rolling and toll processing. Together, these capabilities allow Worthington to shape and refine steel to meet customers' needs with the highest degree of accuracy.

Worthington diversification began in 1980 when it purchased Buckeye International and moved into the steel castings and custom plastics markets. In 1983, the company entered the *Fortune* 500. More recent expansions into automotive aftermarket body panels, suspended ceiling markets and residential steel supporters have cemented Worthington's commitment to the steel processing and metals-related businesses.

In corporate America, the Worthington name is synonymous with success. Profitable in each year of its existence, Worthington has been recognized three times among the 100 best companies to work for in America. Worthington survived the steel industry's lean years without laying off a single worker, all the while boasting an astonishing record of employee productivity.

Much of this is possible because of Worthington's unique relationship with the men and women who work for the company. Worthington fosters camaraderie among workers and, in turn, enjoys an admirable degree of loyalty. As the 1993 edition of *The 100 Best Companies to Work for in America* noted, "One strong testimony to employee satisfaction is the number of longtimers in the original business, steel-processing.... Of the 776 employees in these plants, not counting those that were acquired later, 346, or 44 percent, have been with Worthington for more than 15 years. Forty-seven have been with the company for more than 25 years."

While John H. McConnell has attributed his company's success to "shrewd diversification, ... innovation, and a dedication to product quality, customer service, and technical expertise," he places the major credit on "the mother lode of human relations."

Consequently, Worthington's success cannot be measured only in terms of dollars and percentages — impressive as those numbers are — but also for what Levering and Moskowitz, authors of *The 100 Best Companies to Work for in America*, have called "forward-looking employee practices." Worthington's business philosophy is summed up in the company's Golden Rule, which urges employees to treat all customers, colleagues, investors and suppliers as they would like to be treated. "We concentrate on three basic concepts," McConnell told the Newcomen Society in 1980. "Number one, you have to motivate people. After you motivate them, you have to constantly communicate with them. And then you have to recognize their efforts and give them a pat on the back."

Worthington does this in a number of ways, including perks such as inexpensive haircuts on company time and unlimited coffee breaks, quarterly cash incentives, salaried production workers, an unbroken no-layoff policy, and employee councils that vote on new hires. The introduction of such nontraditional practices has raised eyebrows in the steel industry, but none can argue with their results.

Today, under the leadership of Chairman and CEO John P. McConnell, son of the founder, Worthington Industries continues to set sales records and focus on its steel operations. Raised in the Worthington environment, John P. McConnell is adapting the philosophies that have made the company successful for the emerging global economy. As Worthington's customers consolidate, they are looking to have their needs met by fewer suppliers located in more places. Worthington will be there, turning raw steel into usable material for customers such as Ford and General Motors, Sears, Honeywell, IBM, Samsonite, Eaton, Xerox, Bissell, Kodak, Bell & Howell, Schwinn, La-Z-Boy, Briggs & Stratton, Texas Instruments, Whirlpool and Harley-Davidson.

From a small basement business in 1955 to a modern global corporation with sales of almost $2 billion, it's tribute well earned when John H. McConnell, now chairman emeritus, describes Worthington Industries as the fulfillment of the American Dream.

ACKNOWLEDGMENTS

RESEARCHING, WRITING AND publishing *The Legend of Worthington* would not have been possible without the effort and guidance of a great many individuals, both inside and outside Worthington.

A very special thanks goes to John H. McConnell, founder and chairman emeritus of Worthington Industries. His valuable contribution to the project gave it a personal flavor and accuracy that would have been impossible to reproduce in any other way. Similarly, a special word of acknowledgment is due John P. McConnell, the current CEO and John H. McConnell's son. His support, encouragement and time were invaluable to reconstructing the story of this very successful company.

Thanks are also extended to John Christie, president and COO, and Don Malenick, who recently retired as president after more than four decades with the company. Other corporate officers who took time from their busy schedules to contribute include John Baldwin, vice president and CFO; Robert Borel, vice president–engineering; Dale Brinkman, vice president–administration and general counsel; Jonathan Dove, chief information officer; Ed Ferkany, executive vice president; Bruce Ruhl, vice president–purchasing; Michael R. Sayre, corporate controller; Mark Stier, vice president–human resources; Bill Dietrich, chairman, Dietrich Industries; Ralph Roberts, president, The Worthington Steel Company; Ken Vagnini, president, The Gerstenslager Company; and Virgil Winland, president, Worthington Cylinder Corporation.

A project of this complexity and magnitude would have been impossible without the unflinching support of the corporate communications department, headed by Cathy Mayne Lyttle, vice president–communications. Sonya Lowmiller, community relations coordinator, also contributed greatly, as did Kathy Watson, executive assistant to John H. McConnell.

A special tribute is due to my energetic and well-organized research assistant, Lisa Allen. Lisa conducted much of the archival research, organized the photos and assembled the original narrative timeline.

Thanks also go to the numerous employees and associates of Worthington Industries, both past and present, including: Jim Ballard, Doc Burnquist, John Cummings, Harold "Butch" Dell, Jack Graf, David Hoag, Tom Hockman, Paul Hocter, Ike Kelley, Pete Klisares, Jack Marsh, James Mason, Ed Pati, Red Poling, Ed Ponko, Stephen Senkowski, Kenny Shane and Dick Whitehead.

And finally, a very special word of thanks to the dedicated staff at Write Stuff. Proofreader Bonnie Freeman and transcriptionist Mary Aaron worked quickly and efficiently. Indexer Erika

Orloff assembled the comprehensive index. Particular gratitude goes to Alex Lieber, executive editor; Melody Maysonet and Jon VanZile, associate editors; Sandy Cruz, senior art director; Jill Apolinario, Rachelle Donley and Dennis Shockley, art directors; Fred Moll, production manager; David Patten and Tony Wall, executive authors; Amanda Fowler, executive assistant; Marianne Roberts, office manager; Mike Monahan, director of sales; Bonnie Bratton, director of marketing; Rafael Santiago, logistics specialist; and Karine Rodengen, project coordinator.

Slightly more than a year into his first steel industry job, John H. McConnell, who grew up in rural West Virginia, joined the Navy. He fought at Iwo Jima and went on to found the nation's premier processor of secondary steel products, Worthington Industries.

CHAPTER ONE

MOM, POP AND A '52 OLDS

1955–1958

"The real history of the world is the story of inventions and trades, engineers and builders and businessmen and merchants.... Kings and generals simply rearrange maps. Investors and businessmen rearrange life itself. They are the backbone of civilization."

— Harry Holiday, Jr., CEO, Armco Inc., in a 1980 speech to the Newcomen Society.[1]

WORTHINGTON INDUSTRIES was founded in a small apartment in Columbus, Ohio. In 1955, a young steel salesman named John H. McConnell set up a telephone on his desk and announced that he was in business. This marked the beginning of a company destined to win renown for its unique approach to management and employee relations, as well as for its extraordinary financial success.

Born on May 10, 1923, McConnell was a native of Pughtown (since renamed New Manchester), West Virginia. The tiny town was located about 30 miles west of Pittsburgh in the northernmost sliver of West Virginia, between Pennsylvania to the east and the Ohio River to the west.

Whether Pughtown deserved to be considered a "town" at the time of McConnell's birth is debatable, as it boasted fewer than 100 residents.[2] McConnell grew up in a house without electricity and no indoor plumbing, yet he described his childhood as "almost heaven."[3] He spent his early years playing on his grandfather's small farm, surrounded by family and friends, where "everybody knew everybody" and crime was virtually nonexistent.[4]

McConnell grew up in the very heart of the American steel industry, living in the Appalachian region, where the industry had been born. Deep beneath the lush hills and plunging cliffs lay rich deposits of coal, limestone and iron ore. Fertile

farmland, easy access to coal and the presence of three rivers — the Ohio, Allegheny and Monongahela — began attracting settlers in the 1800s.

Building of an Empire

These settlers quickly exploited the rich natural resources in the region and, by the 1860s, Pittsburgh had a population of 130,000 and was a major hub of industry.[5] Coal mining and boat building were the mainstays, with planing mills, saw mills, grist mills and brickyards working side by side.[6] Coal fueled the city's growth, turning the air black with smoke. As one observer noted, "Even snow can scarcely be called white in Pittsburgh."[7]

This confluence of large deposits of coal and iron, rivers for transportation and a growing population made Pittsburgh a natural choice to become the center of the steel industry. As industry writer John Hoerr describes, the "beginning of the 1870s was precisely the right time in the industrial development of the United States for the appearance of a steel industry. Iron had

McConnell, pictured around the time he founded The Worthington Steel Company in 1955, had already worked in the mills for Weirton. His company was originally a steel broker.

served its purpose in the early stages of the Industrial Revolution, but the infrastructure for the next great leap — railroads, bridges, factories and office buildings — required a stronger, less malleable material."[8]

It also required an entrepreneurial genius, who arrived in the form of Andrew Carnegie. Carnegie began building his steel empire in the 1870s after steel rails produced by small outfits began threatening his hold on the railroad market.[9] Starting with the Edgar Thomson Works, a steel outfit located eight miles from Pittsburgh on the Monongahela River, Carnegie and his associates transformed the entire region into a steel-making machine.[10]

"Mill buildings were erected, blast furnaces were raised, railroad spurs built. Smoke poured into the skies, and flames leaped from the furnaces. All sorts of mill suppliers moved into the towns, and related industries sprouted along the slices of riverbank not yet gobbled up by the first iron and steel interests."[11]

During the last quarter of the 19th century, Carnegie Steel, through shrewd internal expansion and an aggressive acquisition strategy, gathered its strength together to become, in the words of Hoerr, "a business monolith that had no corporate peer in the 1890s." The company created integrated steel mills that were complete centers of production. For raw materials, it owned coal mines and limestone quarries, purchased huge reserves of iron ore and transported its wealth of resources by a vast network of barges and railcars. In 1892, the company earned about $4 million; eight years later that figure had increased by a factor of ten.[12]

In its zeal to lower production costs, Carnegie Steel also established the tenor of the steel industry. The ambition that allowed the Edgar Thomson plant to lower production costs from $36.52 per ton of steel rail in 1878 to just $12.00 in 1898 "inspired the inventiveness that mechanized the productive operations."

"It selected and hardened the managerial ranks. Its technological and psychological consequences, finally, defined the treatment of the steelworkers.

Long hours, low wages, bleak conditions, anti-unionism flowed alike from the economizing drive that made the American steel industry the wonder of the manufacturing world."[13]

By the turn of the century, Carnegie's Pittsburgh had become a major center of manufacturing, finance and ostentatious, unbridled wealth.[14] The city "had a large concentration of iron works, foundries, glass factories, railroads, boat yards and banks, as well as mansions, theaters and a growing cultural life. Industry had spread northward along the Allegheny [River] and southward along the Monongahela."[15]

Yet the industrial crawl had stopped a few miles from the mouth of the Ohio River, where farmland and small patches of industry dotted the landscape. Pittsburghers considered the residents of these little villages "country people" living on the "other side of a cultural and economic gap."[16]

McConnell: The Early Years

John H. McConnell's hometown was one of these patches. Interspersed among the farmers of this rural area were coal and steel mill workers whose families had immigrated to the region. McConnell's own ancestors had come first to western Pennsylvania, then West Virginia, from Scotland and Ireland.[17] His grandfather was a superintendent in a clay mine that made refractory bricks for the Pittsburgh steel mills.[18] McConnell's father and uncles earned fifty cents an hour working at nearby Weirton Steel.[19]

Life in Pughtown was humble at best, deprived at worst. "We didn't realize how poor we were, but today it would be poverty level or below," McConnell recalled in a commencement address given at Ashland College in 1988. "I was born and raised in a house with no electricity. We had gas lights, no central heat, coal stoves with grates, no telephone and, worst of all, no inside plumbing. But we survived and we were happy."[20]

His early education took place in a two-room schoolhouse that crowded four grades in each room. A potbelly stove in one corner provided the only source of heat during the often fiercely cold winters. Toilet facilities at the school, as in most homes, consisted of outhouses. Yet McConnell describes his childhood as "a good way to grow up," for the gifts of a place like Pughtown rose above material concerns.[21] Growing up among farmers and laborers, he was steeped in a work ethic as strong as the steel flowing out of the Weirton mill. At age 10 he went to work hoeing corn for 10 cents an hour. "Anybody that didn't work was an outcast," he would remark years later. "That's the work ethic we had."[22]

McConnell also recalled his academic performance as being less than stellar. "The high school contained 300 kids. My graduating class in 1941 had 60 students. I was number 38."[23] His academic mediocrity, however, was balanced by athletic prowess — he played every varsity sport except basketball, which he skipped because he didn't want to hitchhike the six miles home after practice in the wintertime.

Athletics provided McConnell's first opportunity to experience life beyond Pughtown. Following his high school graduation in 1941, he was offered a football scholarship at the University of West Virginia in Morgantown. It would have made him the first person on either side of his family to go to college. "Ninety percent of the kids that went through high school went to work; they didn't go to college," remembered McConnell. "That was something that only the wealthy could do."[24]

On the day he had to accept or refuse the scholarship, Weirton Steel offered him a job. "My dad said that if I went to Morgantown and got hurt, don't expect any help because he couldn't give it to me," said McConnell, "which was true."[25] He passed up his chance to see the wider world and went to work in the mill.

McConnell became a steelworker at a good time for the industry. Since the rise of Carnegie Steel, the United States had been the largest producer of steel in the world. In 1946, the United States was responsible for more than 54 percent of global raw steel production.[26] Still following the model laid out by Carnegie, the industry was dominated by integrated steel companies like U.S. Steel, Bethlehem, Inland and National. Together known as "Big Steel," these integrated mills were vertical islands of production. They commanded the complete chain of operations from mining the coal and iron ore to rolling and finishing steel products.

The integrated mills were also protected by an "informal system" of cooperation to manipulate prices and maintain profits. The system was informal, of course, to avoid violating federal antitrust laws, but it had existed since Judge Elbert H. Gary's 1901 to 1927 tenure as chairman of U.S. Steel.[27] Even without the collusion, competing against the integrated mills would have been virtually impossible. For a small company, it would require three separate plants simply to ready the iron for the steel-making process.[28]

From the Production Line to the Firing Line

Weirton, where McConnell took his first steel job, was part of National Steel. It had been formed in 1929 by the merger of three companies including the original Weirton Steel. Weirton's founder, Ernest T. Weir, was one of the "most anti-union of the old generation of steel bosses."[29] Weirton employed more than 15,000 workers and was the largest producer of tin plate in the world.[30] McConnell worked on the electric gang maintaining equipment. Through family members he had been close to the steel industry all his life, but now he received a thorough education. He worked in the blooming mill, where hot ingots are rolled into slabs that are then further reduced to make massive steel coils.[31] Because he was fixing equipment, McConnell learned the various processes involved in large-scale steel production. His future as a steelworker appeared to be cast, as it was almost certain that he would live his life laboring in the mill, as had the generations that came before.

In 1943, however, the demands of history changed McConnell's course. Little more than a year into his job at Weirton, he joined the Navy, spending the next two years on the aircraft carrier USS *Saratoga*, working gunfire control during the Second World War. It was remarkable service typical of the generation that "saved the world." At Iwo Jima, McConnell and his fellow crew members helped keep the *Saratoga* afloat despite taking seven bomb hits.

After war's end, McConnell was due for happier times. He spent a season in Hawaii on a Navy football squad, and on February 8, 1946, one week out of the Navy, he married his high school sweetheart, Peggy Rardin.

BEHIND THE WALLS

THE U.S. STEEL INDUSTRY DOMINATED the world after World War II. It had been created by decades of investment and ingenuity — but no one guessed it was headed for disaster. In fact, the seeds of blight that would later infect the integrated mills had been sown as early as 1950. In general, there are four reasons American Big Steel fell during the mid-1970s and 1980s: the disparity between capacity and consumption, investment in the wrong technologies, labor problems, and the rise of foreign competition.

In 1947, however, fully 57 percent of the world's raw steel was produced in the United States.[1] In the 1950s, when U.S. troops marched into Korea, the federal government pressured steel companies to expand.[2] In *Steel: Upheaval in a Basic Industry*, authors Donald Barnett and Louis Schorsch write:

> "While production exceeded rate capacity in 1951, the year in which this dispute [between the government and steelmakers] was most intense, it did not exceed 95 percent of capacity in any succeeding year. Far from having expanded to an inadequate extent in the 1950s, the U.S. steel industry actually increased capacity substantially in what was essentially a flat market."[3]

Between 1949 and 1959, American steel capacity grew at a compound annual rate of more than 4 percent, while consumption inched along at only 0.4 percent.[4] While these numbers seem ominous, the market looked solid on the surface because of exploding demand for personal goods such as cars, appliances and construction materials. But these products use less steel than the heavy capital goods (railroads, ships, industrial machinery) that had been the mainstay of the industry. Additionally, as lighter gauges of cold-rolled and coated steels became available, the trend toward the use of lighter weight steels began.[5] By 1959, the United States had become the first industrialized country to see the steel intensity of its gross national product decline.[6]

The "unjustified optimism" of the steel industry in the 1950s was further complicated by the rapid growth in Europe and Japan.[7] Japan, in particular, built its own profitable steel industry using new technology including the Basic Oxygen Furnace, which converts the hot metal into molten steel, replacing the open hearth.[8] This technology reduced the time needed to refine steel from more than six hours to less than 40 minutes.[9] In contrast, U.S. companies poured money into the open hearth technology, which became obsolete by 1960.[10] According to *Business Week*, this capital investment program ended up being "40 million tons of the wrong kind of capacity."[11]

While steel executives were realizing their mistake, labor strife — long the bane of the industry — opened the door to foreign competitors. In the first 14 years following World War II, the United Steelworkers union conducted five major strikes against the leading steel producers; the fifth, in 1959, sidelined more than 500,000 steelworkers and 250,000 workers in related industries for 116 days.[12] Buyers faced with dwindling stockpiles imported steel and were pleasantly surprised by it. That year, imports exceeded exports for the first time in the 20th century.[13]

From then on, with each contract negotiation between the Steelworkers and Big Steel, "new surges in imports occurred ... and each time they did not drop back afterward."[14] Shaken, integrated mills began handing out generous contracts. By 1970, the hourly wage of unionized steelworkers was 27 percent higher than the manufacturing average; by 1980, the figure had soared to 67 percent.[15]

Big Steel was pricing itself out of the market it had created.

The young McConnell played a number of varsity sports in high school and went on to play football at Michigan State University as a Spartan. He is number 61, second from left.

The couple soon followed a Navy buddy of McConnell's to Michigan, where McConnell enrolled at Michigan State on the GI Bill. He majored in business, but his most important learning occurred outside the classroom. Indeed, one such business experience helped shape his vision of what his own company would be.

There was a special program for married veterans that allowed them to share night shifts with other students at the Oldsmobile plant in Lansing, Michigan. The work was important but not especially taxing. "We could get production on every machine in there in five hours without even straining," McConnell remembered. "In eight hours you had to do 600 parts or something. We could do it in five hours and not even work hard."[32]

Once their quotas were filled, McConnell and his buddies would break out the textbooks and study, a reasonable and responsible activity for students working their way through college. Reasonable to most, that is.

"General Motors didn't say a word," he recalled. "The foreman didn't say a word. The union stopped us."[33]

Union rules required the men to spread their work over an eight-hour shift so as not to interfere with established worker quotas. McConnell was disturbed by what he felt to be an unnaturally slow factory pace. It was then he decided that if he ever owned his own business, he would encourage workers to do better. He believed that incentives and profit sharing would be good ways to motivate workers and increase production. "A lot of my business philosophy came out of there because of waste," he recalled years later. "I could see waste everywhere."[34]

The experience also instilled in him a distrust of unions. "I think, in the beginning, unions did try to protect their people," McConnell said, "but later on, they drifted away."[35] Too many rules, he felt, interfered with common sense. As an example, he points to another incident at Oldsmobile:

"One night I was running a progressive die, making sway bars, and they had just had this die built. It was a deal where steel came in this end and came out the other end a finished product — bang, bang, bang, progressively through. And it jammed on me and slit the die. Of course they were a little unhappy, but it wasn't me, it was the machine that jammed, and the foreman knew it. But under the union contract, the company had to give me a week off. So, you know, I get a little bitter about unions. I belonged to three or four unions in my life, and none of them ever helped me."[36]

In 1949, McConnell graduated from Michigan State with a degree in business and began looking for a way to support his wife and their baby daughter. Courted by a couple of companies, he asked a former professor for advice on what path his career should follow. "I had interviewed [with Weirton Steel] during the Thanksgiving break," he recalled. "They offered me a job in the sales department starting at $225 a month.... The best advice I ever had I got from that professor. I said, 'Look, I can go with this soap company. They'll pay me $100 a week plus a car. Or I can go back to Weirton Steel at $225 a month.' He said, 'Go back to steel and learn steel. You don't want to sell soap.'"[37]

This was one of the turning points in his life.

Astride the World:
The Dominance of American Steel

The global dominance of the U.S. steel industry in the decade following World War II, around the same time McConnell went back to Weirton, has been compared to "Gulliver's status among the Lilliputians."[38] The steel mills around Pughtown and throughout the Midwest were the heart of the U.S. war machine, dependent as it was on steel for the production of everything from helmets to aircraft carriers. The government had invested heavily in capacity expansion and technological upgrades at the mills. By 1950, American plants were easily the largest, most technologically advanced in a world still recovering from devastation wrought by seven years of world war.[39]

Although the end of the Korean War collapsed the market for military products, a burgeoning period of consumer confidence opened new markets for steel. The automobile, with its sharp fins and shining chrome, was a steadfast symbol of the 1950s. It was also an icon of the steel industry. By 1959, 70 percent of American households owned a car.[40]

Historically, periods of industrial growth — for example, the late 1800s and the 1920s — had been focused on collectively owned capital goods such as railroads, steamships and factories.[41] But as the American economy matured, the market for personal products surged. "In 1947, after the war-time mobilization of the economy had ended," writes steel author Christopher Hall, "the three major industries transforming steel for personal use — automobiles, appliances and canning — used only 24 percent of U.S. steel shipments.

"The bulk went to end uses in construction; defense; agriculture; the newer energy industries of oil, gas and electricity; and traditional heavy industries such as railroads, industrial machinery and equipment, shipbuilding, and mining. By 1959 the product mix had changed. Automobiles and appliance shipments and tinplate now accounted for 31 percent of the total, while flat-rolled steel overall had grown from 39 percent to 52 percent, a proportion that would stay steady into the 1990s."[42]

At Weirton, McConnell was responsible for the Chicago district sales office, working the inside order desk for customers in Chicago, Cincinnati, New York, Rochester and Pittsburgh. The biggest problem he faced was how to keep up with demand. As writers Barnett and Schorsch observed in the 1990s, "It is difficult to recall the dominance enjoyed by the U.S. steel industry in the immediate postwar period. We have become accustomed to portrayals of today's steel industry as plagued by severe competitive problems, faced with persistent decline, and dependent on governmental favors. Yet the competitive strengths and advantages of the U.S. steel industry were very evident as late as the 1960s. Its dominance was touted by both the industry and its critics."[43]

Years later, McConnell would laugh that his job at Weirton was good training in how to think on his feet, juggling the needs of customers with the company's inability to keep up with orders. "I got an invitation one time from a customer in Chicago, inviting me to a birthday party," he said. "I thought, what the hell is going on? I don't know anybody there! So I called them. They said, 'It will be the first anniversary of order number so and so that you still haven't shipped.'"[44]

Just as his experience at the Oldsmobile plant vividly showed him how not to operate a company, his second tenure at Weirton showed him how it should be run. Weirton was a good company to work for because employees had a lot of esprit de corps, fostered by E.T. Weir.[45] McConnell had fond memories of attending company picnics as a child. Now a husband and father himself, he began to appreciate the way the managers at Weirton nurtured a sense of family. "They worked on it," he remembered. "They had a company publication called the *Bulletin*, and all the time I was in the service I got that every month because they kept in touch with all the veterans."[46]

After two years with Weirton, McConnell took a job with a small, independent steel broker in Sharon, Pennsylvania. With about 40 employees, the company was quite a change from the mammoth 15,000-worker plant at Weirton. In 1954, McConnell moved to Columbus, Ohio, and began selling on straight commission. There, the idea that became Worthington Industries was born.

Taking Chances

In the 1950s, the busy steel industry emphasized production: Tonnage shipped was the measure of success, while quality and cost were secondary matters.[47] Conversely, customers of steel companies were requiring more specialized products to meet the growing demand for consumer goods. For an integrated firm like U.S. Steel, supplying customers with small orders of specially processed steel was unprofitable, considering the company's giant capital outlay. With close ties to both customers and suppliers, as well as a working knowledge of equipment, McConnell believed he could fill the gap and saw a niche created by changing times.

"During those years of working in the mill and then calling on steel users," he explained, "I recognized that a niche was developing in the industry, and I believed there would be a growing need for custom steel-processing services. The major producers were building larger mills and moving away from smaller tonnage and more specialized orders."[48]

In 1955, he brokered his first load of steel. The order came from the Ohio Thermometer Company in Springfield, which needed a load of zinc-coated steel. McConnell knew that Weirton had an excess of 140,000 pounds that would fit the bill. Although he lacked cash — his only company assets at the time were the desk and phone in the basement of his apartment — he assumed Weirton would grant him typical 30-day terms.

"I sent the purchase order in to Weirton," he said. "Typed it myself and sent it in. Got a call from the credit manager, who had been a good friend all the time I was there.... He said, 'You've got to send cash in advance because you're not incorporated.' I didn't have it, but I said, 'I'll get it.'"[49]

With just $1,200 in his checking account, McConnell was $600 shy of the purchase price. He jumped in his 1952 Oldsmobile and drove to the City National Bank office on Olentangy River Road in Columbus. By offering his Olds as collateral, he finagled a $600 loan from the bank and completed his sale. Once the order was shipped, he said, "Everybody was happy," and he paid off the loan three weeks later, pocketing a $600 profit.[50]

Encouraged by this beginning, McConnell continued to broker steel, matching the precise needs of a customer with the excess loads of a supplier. He found that many companies had steel lying around that would otherwise go to waste.[51] He began to make a name for himself as a broker willing to work with small, specialized orders. When he traveled, the man whose office consisted of a phone in his basement left his wife, Peggy, in charge of the company. Being in charge meant that Peggy answered the phone.

In 1955, Worthington Steel received its first order for brokered steel. When McConnell tried to order the steel from Weirton, however, he was told he needed to pay in advance. Lacking the money, McConnell took out a loan against his 1952 Oldsmobile to ensure the company's first successful sale.

In 1961, Worthington installed this rolling mill at Columbus. It allowed the company to offer the innovative one-pass processing.

CHAPTER TWO

PEOPLE ARE THE PRODUCT

1959–1967

*"I've never thought about [failure] in my entire life. It has never entered
my mind to this day. When you start with nothing — and I did; I went to
school with cardboard in my shoes — what are you going to lose?"*

— John H. McConnell[1]

OPPORTUNITIES QUICKLY PRE-
sented themselves to the
young company. In spring
1955, McConnell was offered the
chance to do more than buy and sell
steel, but he would have to share the
business with a man from Chicago
named Harry Bollster.

Bollster owned a slitting line. The huge
machine was used to cut coils of steel, often
weighing thousands of pounds, with rotary knives
either for edge trimming or to create narrower
coils. These smaller pieces of steel were further
processed into thousands of products. Bollster
had set the slitter up in an old railcar building
and had begun cutting steel for General Motors.
He wanted McConnell to be his salesman.

The two men formed a company, Michigan
Steel Supply. In the first month, McConnell made
an incredible $10,000, but it soon became appar-
ent that he and Bollster had different philosophies on how to run a business. Bollster, whom
McConnell liked and respected, adhered to a conservative view of business; McConnell, on the
other hand, possessed the enthusiasm of youth
and the purpose of someone who had experienced
the old way and believed he could do better. The
two parted as friends in June 1955, and
McConnell struck out on his own.[2]

Immediately after quitting the partnership,
McConnell incorporated The Worthington Steel

Company. The tiny company
started with no cash reserves
and no equipment, leading McConnell
to remark years later, "I think you could
safely say we were undercapitalized."[3]

He soon found two investors, however: Bill Rogers and Del Palmer, themselves partners in the Columbus Stamping
Company. Rogers and Palmer were willing to
match the $5,000 McConnell put in.[4] They also
arranged for the purchase on credit of a 36-inch
slitting line with motor generators. The price of
the slitter and generators was $53,000.[5]

That summer, Margaret Orth was hired as
Worthington Steel's first employee.[6] "In the beginning I was secretary, bookkeeper, you name it,"
she later said.[7]

As they waited for the slitting machine to
arrive, McConnell spent the summer months buying and selling steel. While waiting, Worthington
bled money slowly, and McConnell's partners were
getting impatient. "We had lost from June to
September about $3,000 because I was still just
brokering," McConnell said. "And these guys
wanted out."[8]

Worthington Steel grew quickly in its first years of operation. By
the early 1960s, the company had started expanding the
Columbus plant far beyond its original 16,000 square feet.

At first, Palmer and Rogers offered to buy out McConnell, saying they had found another man who knew how to run the slitter. McConnell doubted it. "I said, 'Well, hell, you don't know the business. What would you do with this?'" he recalled later.[9]

Uncertain where he would locate the funds, McConnell instead offered to buy them out and began looking for investors again. This time, he found help close to home. His new investment group included McConnell's father-in-law, Porter Rardin, and other relatives.

The slitter arrived in September, and McConnell spent the first nights drilling holes in the floor of the building, which he rented from Palmer and Rogers.[10] He set up the machine, poured in the hot lead and set the bolts himself; the only construction project he hired out was the electrical wiring. A week and a half after the slitter became operational, the $3,000 loss had been erased.[11]

Suddenly, his old investors wanted to stay in. "I kept telling them, 'After we get the slitter running,

Worthington Steel's first slitting line. This 36-inch slitting machine cost $53,000 and was several months late in delivery. When it did come, John H. McConnell set up the machine himself.

Inset: The company's first plant, which was leased from McConnell's first investors.

we're going to be fine,'" he remembered. "So when they decided they didn't want to sell out, I said no."[12]

Part of the deal to buy out the old partners required McConnell to lease the 7,000-square-foot building and do their slitting free for five years.[13] As things turned out, this was a small price to pay. In its first year of business, with five employees working one machine, The Worthington Steel Company earned a modest $14,000 profit on sales of $350,000.[14] The next year, sales and earnings dipped slightly to $342,000 and $11,000, respectively. In 1957, however, the company began a rapid upward trajectory.[15] That year, sales more than doubled to $699,000, with earnings of $22,000.[16]

In the company's first few years, John McConnell could count the number of employees on his fingers. Ed Pati, who joined Worthington in 1957 at age 20, was one of them:

"I was introduced to Worthington by a mutual friend. I came down here as a trial, if you will, or just to see what it would be like. I liked it. I saw potential in Mr. McConnell, number one. I liked John, and I liked what he stood for. The more I got to know John McConnell and the more I saw what was going on and the way he treated people, the more I liked it."[17]

This emphasis on the worker/company relationship distinguished Worthington from its earliest days. Everyone — including John McConnell himself — was a laborer; and everyone — including the machinists and laborers — was a salesman.

"It was a situation in which the core people did what they thought they had to do," said Pati.

"There were no boundaries between departments. Mr. McConnell believed deeply in the fact that you don't have anything unless you have an order, and anybody could take an order. If somebody called here after hours and you happened to

---

After Worthington cut steel to a specific size and thickness, the coils were banded and shipped to customers. One of the nation's first specialty processors, Worthington quickly developed a reputation for quality products.

be working late, and the guy was in trouble, you did what you had to do to try to help him out."[18]

Dick Whitehead, whose service with Worthington began in 1959, was also struck by the company's informal nature. Hired to "sweep floors, band steel or just labor," Whitehead said he worked alongside Porter Rardin, the company's vice president and principal investor. "He would just work with everybody else," Whitehead remembered. "Nobody knew who he was. They just thought he was a janitor, but he was probably the guy cutting more [steel] than anybody."[19]

This attitude towards hierarchy became an early and important part of the corporate culture. All individuals within the organization were valued for the practical contribution they made to the overall business, rather than for their position on the corporate ladder, which would have been rather small in the late 1950s, but which was growing quickly.

Worthington quickly became a successful business. The company pushed its single slitter beyond capacity. It was designed to pull only four cuts at three-sixteenths-inch thickness off 12,000-pound coils.

"We overloaded that thing quite a

bit," McConnell said. "I remember times when we had maybe ten cuts on it."[20]

Worthington also began to distinguish itself in the kind of business it pursued. Unlike larger steel companies that offered large-lot steel processing, Worthington courted the small, highly specialized orders. For United Technologies, located in Zanesville, Ohio, Worthington supplied steel for electronic controls and flat-rolled automotive products such as door trim, locks and bracketing. Inland Fisher Guide, another early customer, ordered steel for special-cut automotive products like trim and door frame. Pax Machine of Celina, Ohio, needed oil-filter topping plates.[21]

On another occasion, McConnell recalled visiting the General Electric facility in Louisville. GE needed an order of steel cut to precise specifica-tions, three-sixteenths of an inch thick and three feet long with a rounded edge, and it needed it fast. McConnell assured the GE manager he could do it, but when he got back to the factory, his production manager said it would take at least a week to run the order. So, after finishing his sales rounds, McConnell changed into work clothes and prepared to work all night.

It is worth remembering that McConnell was operating this slitter before automation had reached steel processing; the work was exhausting. The giant coils often weighed as much as 40,000 pounds (approximately 20 times the weight of a modern automobile), and it could take several men to feed the tail of the coil into the slitter.[22]

"I was about to die," McConnell remembered of that night. "Sweat was rolling off of me. They sent

THE LONGEST DAY

WHEN DESCRIBING HIS COMPANY'S early successes, McConnell often told a story he heard growing up in West Virginia:

"Two people strolling on a country lane and see a turtle resting on top of a fence post.

"'You know how that turtle got on that fence post?' one asks.

"'No,' the other replies.

"'Somebody put it there,' answers the first."[1]

The turtle, McConnell would point out, didn't get to the top alone.

Don Malenick is one Worthington leader who readily admits to getting plenty of help along the way. Malenick started working at Worthington in 1958 as a 19-year-old general laborer, and was typical of the early crop of employees. One of seven children, he was the son of a West Virginia coal miner who never made more than $6,000 a year. After high school, Malenick, unable to afford college, worked as a meat cutter, married his high school sweetheart and moved to Chicago briefly to take a job at Inland Steel.[2] For a country boy, moving to the big city was like "going from heaven to hell," so he happily accepted a job at Worthington.[3]

He has vivid memories of what steel processing was like in the days before automation. Workers had to physically manhandle huge coils of steel, and the work could be backbreaking.

"When I came to Columbus, I rented a sleeping room, and I had to pay seven dollars a night," he recalled. "I went to work at Worthington on Monday, and when I went back to my room that evening, I was so damn tired, every muscle in my body ached. I thought, 'This is not going to get easier.' I thought, 'I'm just going to take a shower and get in my car and drive back to West Virginia. I'm not even going to spend the night.'"[4]

But something about his day made him think twice. He decided to go out for a sand-wich, then came back to the room: "I thought, 'I'll go to bed and just get up and go back to the hills of West Virginia the next morning.' I went

a guy back to help me finally, and we got it down to GE."[23] Worthington had won itself another loyal customer, and John McConnell had provided a vivid, real-life example of his driving philosophy.

"He could handle most of everything," Pati said. "He did all the purchasing himself. I don't know what year it was, somewhere around 1966, 1967, 1968, that I was helping him do it. He'd make the decision and I'd do the paperwork."[24]

Similarly, Dick Whitehead remembered McConnell's all-encompassing approach to the business.

"Mr. McConnell used to stay out and try to sell steel during the day, and maybe we'd be getting ready to go home and you'd get a phone call. He'd promised something for the next morning, so

you had to stay and get it done. If something broke down, he would work on it.... I can remember him sweating with that big, bald head with grease all over it."[25]

Sharing in the Success

Worthington's philosophy encompassed more than hard work; McConnell was building a company on a web of personal relationships and an attitude shaped by camaraderie and a certain informality. Sports, for instance, had always been a large part of McConnell's life, and that was carried into the business. The workers often gathered to play softball. On slow days, some of the men pocketed their paychecks and took off for lunch at a "beer joint," as Whitehead recalled. "But they'd be

---

to bed. 'Well,' I thought, 'I'll set the alarm clock and see how I feel in the morning. I may go to work, and then I'll drive back that evening.'"[5]

The next morning, Malenick decided his body could withstand at least one more day. Although his muscles didn't fare any better, he began to notice the way Worthington was run. He was impressed.

At Inland Steel, Malenick had been a member of the union.

"That was the most disgusting thing I ever saw in my life," he said. "I probably worked, at the most on a busy day, two hours out of eight, and I would get bored.... I would see some of the people in the mill working really hard, so I'd go over and say, 'Let me give you a break because I want something to do.'... I would throw three shovels of slag or something, and all of a sudden, somebody would tap me on my shoulder and say, 'That's not your job. Put the shovel down, get the hell out of here.' That was the union."[6]

Like McConnell, Malenick was irritated by union rules that seemed to defy common sense. "We had a little maintenance shop that I worked out of, and if we had lightbulbs on the shelf, I couldn't get on a ladder and change that

lightbulb. I had to call the Electrical Group, and they would send two electricians up there [to] change that lightbulb, then sit around and BS for half an hour."[7]

What Malenick saw at Worthington was the way he believed American companies should be run. "They talked to you," he said. "They treated you like you were a human being or a part of the company, not just another number. I think part of the problem [at Inland] was the fact that the people there thought they worked for the union. They didn't work for the company. Here, from management to employees to laborers, everyone works together as a team. That was a big difference in the environment."[8]

So, on the third day, Malenick again dragged his sore body out of bed to punch the Worthington time clock, and the next day he went back. And again and again. Over the next two decades, he would rise through the ranks from a helper on a machine to an operator to a supervisor to plant superintendent.

In 1976, Don Malenick, the man who had rested his aching bones in a Columbus hotel room 18 years before and had seriously thought about quitting, became the president of the corporation.

back at work Saturday morning because they were broke. We worked hard and we played hard."[26]

In 1958, just three years old and with fewer than a dozen workers, Worthington Steel became a $1 million company in sales, with earnings of $24,000.[27] While the company employees were definitely pleased, it was only the beginning of what John H. McConnell envisioned, and ultimately his vision had little to do with size. Being the largest company of its type was not necessarily his goal. With only a handful of employees and a lone piece of equipment, that seemed pretty unlikely anyway. But McConnell did want his company to be the best company in its industry. He encouraged his workers to take pride and ownership in their work. If growth was the result, then so be it.

And grow Worthington did. In 1959, the 20-member staff of Worthington Steel posted sales of just over $2 million and earnings of $49,000, more than double the previous year.[28] That year, Worthington Steel purchased two acres north of Columbus and built a 16,000-square-foot plant.[29] The irony, as McConnell would recall 10 years later, was that "We wondered what we would do with all that space."[30]

This growth happened despite a massive labor strike in the steel industry that idled Big Steel's production for 116 days through the summer and fall of 1959.[31] The strike had been expected and rippled through the national economy. Coming at the end of a three-year contract cycle for the United Steelworkers of America, it was the fifth major work stoppage in a 13-year period. Steel customers like Worthington had stockpiled reserves in anticipation of a shutdown.[32]

Worthington faced some dry months, which were shared by the employees, who earned monthly bonuses based on tonnage shipped. Whitehead got a check for only seven dollars one month, and to make matters worse, he said, "Don Malenick, another Worthington employee, was going around taking them up. He was going to give them back" to

help the struggling company.[33] Whitehead, who had just joined Worthington, held on to his check.

When the strike finally ended, business soared. "Anything you had in here you could sell," said Whitehead.[34] To meet the order backlog, Worthington offered workers as many hours as they could handle. Whitehead showed up at 7 a.m. Thanksgiving Day and cut steel until 3 p.m. the following day to fill an order.[35] "I may have made a hundred bucks that week," he said. "And I was making $1.40 an hour."[36]

Four years after being founded, Worthington purchased this plant in Columbus, Ohio. Although it seemed too large to fill at first, Worthington almost immediately outgrew the new facility.

Scioto Metals

In 1959, with the strike still going on, McConnell branched out and formed Scioto Metals, an affiliate of Worthington Steel that would fill the needs of large and small manufacturers for special alloys and for basic non-ferrous products such as aluminum, copper and brass.[37] At the time, these metals were in ever-increasing demand for the manufacture of space exploration and aircraft products as well as more conventional items such as display cases and trimming.

Initially, Scioto Metals distributed only brass and aluminum sheet but soon expanded operations to include slitting, shearing, roller leveling, sawing and cutting special metals into various shapes and forms. Among the industries it served were automotive, appliance, aircraft, heating and cooling, defense, construction, electronics, and transportation.[38]

The foundation for rapid expansion at Worthington had been established, and in the early 1960s two trends emerged that helped strengthen Worthington's position in the fledgling processing industry. First, the strong performance of the U.S. economy created a steel boom that lasted into the mid-1960s.[39] Second, a new kind of steel producer emerged on the scene.

The steel boom was good for Worthington because it caused the major mills to pour their profits into expensive development of open-hearth technology. This, in turn, caused them to concentrate on larger customers and forsake the smaller, specialty processing orders that Worthington thrived on.[40] Unlike the larger companies, which were scrambling to retain their dominance over the world steel industry, Worthington's style was to work closely with customers on unique orders, calling on them directly, determining exactly what they needed in terms of tolerance, chemistry and quantity, then figuring out a way to meet the need.

The response to this approach was so overwhelming that McConnell often spent his day making sales calls at companies like Westinghouse and Fisher Body and his nights working the equipment alongside his employees. His affable personality, sales acumen and general knowledge of steel got him in the door, but it was Worthington's commitment to stay "exceptionally attuned to the customer's needs" that won orders.[41]

The Minimill

No matter how much money the big mills poured into their plants, however, a new kind of mill was emerging that heralded a revolution in the steel industry. This new production center was called a minimill.

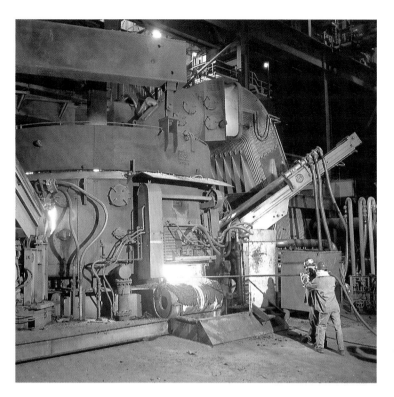

Pictured is an electric arc furnace used at Nucor Corporation. This kind of furnace fueled the growth of the highly efficient minimill. *(Photo courtesy of Nucor Corporation.)*

In the 1930s, the Northwestern Steel and Wire Company had become the first to use electric furnaces solely for carbon steel to produce low-value products like common grades of wire rod, concrete-reinforcing bar and merchant bar.[42] This small, independent mill, based in Sterling, Illinois, was successful in a market from which the integrated mills had begun to retreat.[43] In the 1960s, other companies followed Northwestern's lead.

Twenty-two minimills were built between 1955 and 1969.[44] The term "minimill" referred to any small electric arc furnace mill — independent from integrated mills — that supplied regional markets with low-end products and operated with the lowest possible costs.[45] Electric arc furnace technology produced steel from scrap rather than iron ore, eliminating the need for the expensive coke ovens and blast furnaces.[46]

Starting in the late 1950s, minimills gradually pushed Big Steel out of the commodity-grade

product lines: wire rods, concrete reinforcing bars, bar-size light shapes and hot-rolled bars.[47] By the early 1960s, a dramatic realignment was taking place in the steel industry.

To some degree, this caused Worthington supply problems even as it helped attract customers. As integrated mills sought larger customers themselves, they tended to ignore Worthington, which was still relatively small in terms of tonnage.

"The problem in those days was getting the right material out of the mills because most didn't want to sell if you were too small," McConnell remembered.[48] At first, Weirton was a main supplier, but as Worthington's reputation spread, companies like Bethlehem and J&L began to do business. On what he thought would be one of the biggest days of his life, McConnell got a call from a sales manager at the Columbus office of U.S. Steel. The manager wanted to pay him a visit. Thinking U.S. Steel was about to become a supplier, McConnell believed Worthington was entering the big league.

When the sales manager arrived, however, McConnell realized he wasn't being called up to the big show yet. "He came out because they had a man, Les Worthington, who was going to be promoted to Pittsburgh as vice president of marketing," he said. "They wanted to make sure that Les Worthington wasn't one of the owners at Worthington Steel."[49]

Five Years and Growing

In 1960, the company posted its fifth straight year of profitability and was looking to expand. "I've never thought about failure in my entire life. It has never entered my mind to this day," McConnell has said. "When you start with nothing — and I did; I went to school with cardboard in my shoes — what are you going to lose?"[50]

The company had moved into its new 16,000-square-foot plant only one year earlier, but already the building was inadequate. Worthington doubled the size of the facility and hosted its first open house for customers and suppliers in September of that year.[51]

In 1961, Worthington expanded its facilities by another 14,000 square feet, entirely occupying the original two-acre site.[52] Hoping to expand into

Above: Two years after buying Columbus, Worthington bought a warehouse and distribution center in Louisville, Kentucky. Pictured, from left to right, are Wally Hoops, Vic Wright and Jerry Bisig, part of the startup team.

Below: At the Columbus plant, Worthington's growing operation soon needed a fleet of trucks to deliver product to customers throughout the Midwest.

the fast-growing Southern market, the company also purchased a warehouse/service center in Louisville, Kentucky, chosen for its proximity to large appliance manufacturers and a number of roll-forming companies.[53] From Louisville, Worthington could supply steel to customers in Alabama, Illinois, Indiana, Kentucky, Mississippi and Tennessee. Daily truck routes were set up between Columbus and the Louisville branch, which was located at 1152 Industrial Boulevard on the city's south side.[54]

Although Louisville marked the company's first geographic expansion, sales in 1961 fell to $2.5 million, and earnings plummeted from $122,000 to just $19,000. The purchase drained Worthington's reserves.[55]

The One-Pass

It might have been a hard year for the young business, but it was an important one. In 1961, Worthington installed its first rolling mill and created a market niche that would prove to be its "ride to the future."[56] The new mill was not a full-scale cold rolling mill — the company would not have heavy reduction capabilities until 1982.[57] Instead, McConnell and his engineers custom-designed the new mill to produce a steel product that was a cross between hot and cold rolled. The "one-pass" innovation was born.

Hot rolled steel was created by pushing heated slabs through a series of rolls at increasing speeds, reducing the thickness and lengthening

the slabs into sheets that are rolled into heavy coils. In contrast, cold rolling was a multistep process: Steel coils that had been hot rolled were pickled in an acidic bath to remove scale; oiled to retard oxidation; squeezed through another series of rolls at room temperature or colder to reduce thickness, improve surface finish and increase strength; annealed (a controlled heating process) to reduce the brittleness caused by the cold rolling; and finally, run through a temper mill to provide desirable surface properties (such as galvanized steel or tinplate).[58]

Since cold rolled steel provided a consistency in thickness and workability, it was used for steel products that had to meet close gauge tolerances.

Worthington's one-pass innovation was able to meet the needs of customers who required the consistent gauge controls of cold reduction but not its high-finish characteristics. On the average, one-pass strip was 10 percent to 15 percent less expensive than standard cold rolled strip steel.[59] Also, one-pass held very close tolerances since only a 5 percent reduction was made in a single pass on hot rolled pickled and oiled steel sheet.[60] One-pass gave customers both a better tolerance and a more competitive price.[61]

McConnell had first seen something like the one-pass at Weirton, where a sales vice president suggested that a customer, in select circumstances, would never know whether an order for cold rolled steel had been completely processed.[62] Weirton "couldn't keep up on their cold rolled product," McConnell remembered. "So this guy said, 'Well, take some hot roll. Pickle it. Give it one pass for gauge. Ship it to them. Charge them the cold rolled price.'"[63]

At Worthington, McConnell talked a local customer, Fisher Body Plant, into trying the one-pass. Fisher made locks that required a close gauge in order for the two parts of the lock to match without rattling. The buyer at Fisher tentatively submitted an order, which Worthington priced halfway between the rates for hot rolled and cold rolled strip. Worthington bought a coil of hot rolled steel, slit it, then single-strand rolled it through the mill for gauge control without completing the finish. Fisher was thrilled with the steel — and the savings; the buyer received a raise with the money Fisher had saved.

Worthington was the only company, large or small, that offered customers the one-pass process. Orders trickled in at first; then they poured in. Because one-pass cold rolled strip was particularly suited for a painted or plated product where basic appearance was not of primary importance, sales to the auto industry grew rapidly.[64]

Even more importantly, one-pass made the Worthington name synonymous with innovation. In the five years it took for other companies to copy the process, it solidified Worthington's reputation for excellent value and customer service.[65] The next time Big Steel called, it would be to do business.

Pulling Ahead

With one-pass processing entering the marketplace, Worthington recovered handily from the previous year's slump. Sales for 1962 surpassed $3.2 million.[66] The facilities at Columbus now totaled 52,000 square feet and included three slitting lines as well as a new rolling mill.[67]

That year, Doc Burnquist, an acquaintance of the McConnell family and friend of Porter Rardin, moved from McConnell's native Pughtown to join Worthington. Burnquist began working on the slitting line in Columbus. "Everybody used first names," Burnquist recalled. "And there were times Mr. McConnell came out in the plant. I remember one time we were putting a new slitter in and he was out there helping with it."[68]

Worthington was also busy installing other equipment to help it produce high-quality product. To improve its ability to provide very close tolerance steel, Worthington became one of the first processors in the nation to install an Accu-Ray Strip Thickness Measuring System.[69] Using small amounts of radiation, the Accu-Ray system continuously measured the steel as it was being shaped, lending a higher quality and better control.

In 1963, spurred by a booming auto industry, both the Columbus and Louisville plants were beehives of activity.[70] Trucks arrived hourly at the two docks at Louisville to pick up rolled, coiled, cut and processed steel or deliver tons of coils for inventory and processing.[71] In October, construction at Louisville was started to provide an extra 8,400 square feet for the installation of additional slitting equipment and an automatic banding machine.[72]

These master coils, after slitting by Worthington, are being loaded on a truck at Columbus for shipment to a variety of customers. Worthington steel was used in hundreds of consumer products.

Sales at Louisville were headed by Bill Williams, while General Manager Robert Wheeler oversaw ordering, processing and shipping and worked closely with Worthington Steel's executive vice president, Merwin Ray.[73] Customers serviced by the plant were able to draw from an inventory exceeding 7,000 tons of steel, with special alloys and widths available from the main headquarters at Columbus.[74] Although neither of Worthington's plants offered complete finishing services, the company carried inventory that included a variety of tempers and finishes, including electrolytic zinc, galvanized, cold rolled, and hot rolled pickled and oiled sheet steel in widths up to 54 inches.[75]

Sales for 1963 climbed again, exceeding $3.8 million with earnings of $55,000.[76] An article by Executive Vice President Merwin Ray appeared in the company newsletter and indicated how valuable Worthington Steel was becoming to its customers. Ray recounted an "interesting conversa-tion" he'd had with a buyer who began purchasing from Worthington in 1955:

"Over a cup of coffee, he commented that in 1955 his company carried a steel inventory in excess of $50,000. Today this buyer's company has reduced its dollar inventory in steel to less than $12,500 ... because of the fast, dependable delivery of steel from our plant here in Columbus."[77]

It was clear that The Worthington Steel Company was doing something right. It celebrated its 10th anniversary in 1965 by nearly doubling sales and earnings from the previous year.

Sales surpassed $8.39 million, up from $4.5 million in 1964; earnings rose to $157,000 from only $73,000 one year earlier.[78] The company employed 86 people working two 10-hour shifts six days a week. That schedule enabled the company to process between 4,000 and 5,000 tons of steel every month.[79]

"Ten years have seen much happen at Worthington Steel," McConnell wrote to his employees in *MetalPhonics*, the company newsletter. "The struggle for business as an infant company — the efforts to obtain steel during strikes — the need for additional warehousing — the capital required for inventory, machinery and warehousing — the swing of the pendulum from insufficient business to too much demand — these are among the problems that have confronted us from time to time."[80]

In the late 1960s, Worthington purchased an additional five acres on Huntley Road near the Columbus plant. The facility then had almost 100,000 square feet of production space and was still growing.

McConnell maintained a brisk pace of capital investment. Worthington Steel–Louisville was equipped with additional office and warehousing space, bringing its total square footage to 27,000.[81] At Columbus the company purchased an additional five acres on Huntley Road, bringing the total size of the facilities up to 94,000 square feet.[82]

In 1967, Don Malenick was named vice president of manufacturing and given responsibility for the Ohio facilities, including the Scioto Metals Division.[83] Sales that year topped $12.5 million with earnings of $252,000, and Worthington Steel headed into 1968 with confidence.[84] Although it was a contract year for the big Steelworkers union, Worthington established strong relationships with nonstriking mills and adequate storage space in the event of a strike. The company also initiated a series of monthly seminars for steel buyers that included presentations on purchasing, inspection and production.[85] Buyers were assured that Worthington's "strategic position in the steel industry as a major processor and distributor of steel and other precision-cut metal products will, in the event of a steel short-

Worthington Steel approached its employee relations differently from the typical steel company. Among its benefits, Worthington offered inexpensive haircuts in a company barbershop. Although this particular barbershop closed in the 1980s, a company-sponsored shop remains at Columbus.

age, enable [it] to continue in its usual customer service," saving its customers the exorbitant cost of stockpiling steel.[86]

Shave and a Haircut ...

At more than a decade old and growing quickly, by 1967 Worthington was already gaining a reputation in Columbus as a great company to work for. Keeping his workers happy was an issue

on which McConnell refused to split hairs, and he believed in offering bonuses and incentives. In its first years, Worthington workers were rewarded for how many tons of steel were shipped.

This was a novel enough idea in the traditional steel industry, but it was only one element of McConnell's program. In 1961, he began offering another benefit that meant a lot to employees. "I got tired of having to wait at barbershops and get appointments, so I talked to a local barber to see if he'd be interested in coming in once a week," McConnell said.[87]

Getting a inexpensive haircut on company time was "a heck of a benefit," according to Pati. "We worked long hours, and by the time you'd come home and try to run down to the barbershop to get a haircut, if there was anybody there in front of you there wasn't enough time to get it. Free coffee, too, that was a nice touch, but the haircut, at that time, meant a lot to me."[88]

When he began inexpensive haircuts on company time, McConnell had no idea his management style would one day be required reading at Harvard University.[89] "My business philosophy is not complicated or perhaps not even very sophisticated by business school standards," he said in 1980.[90] "We concentrate on three basic concepts. Number one, you have to motivate people. After you motivate them, you have to constantly communicate with them. And then you have to recognize their efforts, give them a pat on the back in various ways."[91]

McConnell's record on employee relations would later make his company the envy of the steel industry. Worthington Industries was included in every edition of *The 100 Best Companies to Work for in America* and lauded in publications such as *Forbes* and *Fortune*. Tom Peters, author of *A Passion for Excellence: The Leadership Difference*, cited Worthington as a "role model" for other companies to follow.[92]

"It's not what Worthington makes that counts," wrote *Forbes* magazine in 1993. "It's how it runs its business. The company epitomizes good management."[93]

The credit for this widespread enthusiasm about Worthington's management goes to the unassuming McConnell. "He's the kind of person I think anybody would like to work for," remarked Don Malenick.[94] Long before "teamwork" and "total quality management" became buzzwords in business circles, John McConnell understood how to get the most out of the people he worked with.

"He was a leader," said Harold Poling, former CEO of Ford Motor Company and a customer of Worthington's. "I think he became a leader because of his background, and he wanted individuals to feel the success of the company. He felt it was important that they be participants in it."[95]

As McConnell would often point out later, his approach was based on treating people the way he wished to be treated. He held two core beliefs: that workers who were treated with respect and given more responsibility would prove themselves equal to any task; and that corporate policies and union rules generally served to "restrict rather than guide."[96]

Worthington's Golden Rule

So in the earliest days of Worthington Steel, McConnell adopted a single corporate policy that would supersede all others. A variation on the Golden Rule, the Worthington Industries philosophy fits on one small card that all employees

were asked to carry, and the most central statement reads: "We treat our customers, employees, investors, and suppliers as we would like to be treated."[97]

As basic as the idea seems, its practical application proved innovative, even radical, in the conservative business atmosphere of the time. In designing a loose corporate structure that emphasized teamwork and accountability, McConnell collapsed the traditional layers between the factory floor and executive offices.

"Basically," explained his son, John P. McConnell, "my father wanted to set something up where the hourly workforce wasn't set apart from the salaried workforce. Everything he did was kind of geared along those lines."[98]

In the company's infancy, when McConnell rolled up his sleeves and worked the slitter himself, following the Golden Rule was easy. "It just came natural," he said. "You don't cheat. You don't lie. You help your neighbor. All of that was part of it."[99]

After 1960, as the company enjoyed rapid growth, McConnell wanted to ensure that the "us and them" mentality he had encountered between workers and managers in his own employment history did not infect his company.[100] He devised ways to make Worthington a team and to let workers share in the success of their labor. He spent part of every day on the factory floor, long after Worthington was big enough that he no longer had to work the slitters himself, and could often be found chewing tobacco with workers and shooting the breeze.

"I remember one day when it was really hot and Mr. McConnell came driving through the shop in his golf cart with coolers of pop on the back," said Dennis Bentz, whose 29-year career at Worthington began in 1966. "He went through handing pop out to everybody. That makes you feel good. You're not just a piece of equipment."[101]

McConnell "never separated himself from labor," Malenick told the authors of *The 100 Best*

Worthington Industries' philosophy was printed on handy business cards and distributed among its employees. The idea was to develop a framework simple enough to be committed to memory and unambiguous. The cards also featured Worthington's Golden Rule.

Companies to Work for in America. "He's always kept that informal environment that makes it easier for people to work together as a group."[102]

The Salary Structure

Perhaps McConnell's most radical departure from tradition was his approach to compensation. During his time as a factory worker, McConnell had never understood why administrative employees were salaried while the plant workers — the people who could really "put it on the bottom line" — were paid by the hour.[103] So, in 1966, Worthington Steel did away with time clocks and put all employees on salary, complete with paid absences.

Analysts and others in the steel industry said it would never work.[104] But McConnell believed in the integrity of the people he'd hired. "You have to trust the workforce," he said.

"If you don't, you've done an awfully bad job. There are always going to be some you never trust; there are always a few con men around who will take advantage of anything they can find. But, by and large, American workers will do a job if motivated. The work ethic is still there, and to me, it's management's job to get that out."[105]

Trust, McConnell believed, was a form of motivation. Rather than establishing regular coffee breaks, Worthington provided free coffee and other beverages all the time, and workers were told to take breaks whenever they wanted.

"We tell them we are not going to shut down a machine just because it's 10:00 A.M. or whatever. This method says to people, 'You are a responsible person. When you feel you have the time, help yourself,'" said McConnell. "It recognizes people as a valuable part of the team who are trusted to know when a job needs to be done and when a break is appropriate. Our people enjoy this kind of freedom."[106]

Beginning in 1955, Worthington paid bonuses based on tons of steel shipped. This award was paid in cash in addition to an employee's regular paycheck.[107] But by the mid-1960s, as the company moved into producing very close-tolerance, one-pass steel, Worthington needed a program that would encourage production without forsaking quality.

"Our product line had become much more sophisticated, so quality of workmanship became a more important consideration," McConnell said. "And at the same time we realized that since we were also building a reputation around fast, efficient service, we had to provide incentive for the employees to react to customers' needs."[108]

In 1966, Worthington switched to an incentive plan that rewarded bottomline profit.[109] McConnell fixed the portion of pretax profit that would be paid out to employees at 17 percent, a number that remained in place for the next three decades.

"I came on in 1963," remembered Kenny Shane, who joined on the factory floor and retired decades later as vice president of steel manufacturing.

"I think we paid half our medical insurance, and production got a bonus once a month. As the company grew, we didn't have to pay our medical. The next step was profit sharing. When we had the monthly bonus, everybody was working so we could keep that bonus nice, and then when we got profit sharing, everybody worked together because they knew the better they worked, the better the profit-sharing check would be. I always felt that helped to keep the teamwork going because everyone was working to the same end."[110]

John P. McConnell further explained his father's reasoning:

"He had always thought incentive was a good idea, but he also realized that he was paying a bonus on steel that occasionally got rejected and came back in the door — he didn't earn money on it but had paid a bonus on it. So that led him to think about bottom-line profits and sharing it that way.... He arrived at the 17 percent figure by looking at the last tonnage bonus paid and deciding how much it took to make sure the payment was higher."[111]

The elder McConnell set up five participating groups who would share the general pool: production, administrative, truck drivers, maintenance and sales. Each group received a part of the total profit-sharing pool, which was then to be divided among the members of the group according to base salary.[112]

THE EMPLOYEE COUNCIL

"One could argue that in a truly democratic workplace workers would have the right to vote on whether to accept someone into the company. If the idea sounds far-fetched, you haven't been to Worthington Industries."

—Robert Levering and Milton Moskowitz, authors of *The 100 Best Companies to Work for in America.*[1]

FIRST IMPLEMENTED IN THE MID-1960s, along with the profit-sharing plan, the council promotes communication. All Worthington plants, other than union shops brought in through acquisitions, have used employee councils for decades to act as go-betweens for workers and supervisors. The councils are comprised of nonmanagement employees who serve two-year terms. Council members are kept informed of business developments, problems and management goals. They report to their coworkers, who are encouraged to make suggestions, lodge complaints or raise questions.

According to John H. McConnell, the councils are crucial to both the company's success and the employees' satisfaction. "Some people will never feel comfortable speaking with management no matter what you do to encourage them, but they will open up to their peers," he said. "This way we receive input from many employees."[2]

The employee council also determines who will be given the opportunity to join the Worthington team. Because the success of the salary and profit-sharing plans hinges on the caliber of workers Worthington attracts, the councils give employees a say in who their colleagues will be. New hires are brought in on a temporary basis for about three months, after which the employee council votes on whether to promote the person to regular status, which confers salary and profit-sharing privileges.[3] If candidates aren't approved by a majority, management is alerted to a potential problem, and the decision is made whether to give the candidates additional time or let them go. Thanks to a careful screening and hiring process, that hasn't happened often over the 30-plus years of the program, but the voting helps ensure that only the most energetic and honorable workers join the winning team.

"We explained that this method would reward everyone fairly," John H. McConnell said. "The more money the company made, the more each employee would make, regardless of whether he or she was in production, maintenance, sales or administration."[113]

McConnell didn't stop at profit sharing. He also put control over their work environment directly in the workers' hands. When an employee quit or retired, group members were asked whether a new hire was necessary or whether the group could pick up the slack. Workers were encouraged to look for ways to improve productivity, such as reducing scrap.[114] And, since the reward was tied to salary, employees were encouraged to try to improve their position in the company and take on more responsibility.[115] The program was designed as a cash payout so that employees could see tangible evidence of the company's success.

"We did not think a deferred plan would provide enough incentive or generate the kind of day-to-day dedication we were looking to develop," McConnell said.[116]

During the week of June 13, 1966, Worthington Steel handed out its first round of profit-sharing checks, totaling more than $25,000, to cover the three-month period from March 1 to May 31.[117] *MetalPhonics* presented an overview of the new policy to employees:

"The attractive new profit-sharing policy is expected to substantially increase the income

of all employees.... Also under the new plan, 100 percent of the hospitalization and major medical insurance for employees is now paid by the company. An additional benefit is continuance of regular pay for those who are off work due to sickness or injury until insurance payments begin.

"Mr. McConnell explained that the new, forward-looking policies were instituted to give employees greater responsibility in operation of the company. 'After all,' he said, 'the employees of a company are as much a part of it as the management.'"[118]

In its first three years, the profit-sharing program distributed almost $490,000 to Worthington employees, with more than $235,000 given out in 1968 alone.[119] Over the coming decades, the plan routinely placed Worthington employees near the top of the pay scale in the steel processing industry. Profit-sharing checks typically amounted to 35 to 50 percent of an employee's base pay.[120] By 1980, 14 years after the plan was implemented, Worthington had paid out $30 million to non-management employees.[121] That same year, productivity as measured by sales per employee averaged $225,000 compared to a median level of about $77,000 for the metal manufacturing industry and $63,000 for all industries.[122]

Furthermore, the incentive plan, by automatically cutting the company's labor costs during periods of slow business, eliminated the wage rigidity that forced unionized companies to resort to layoffs.[123]

Benefits Falling into Place

Soon after announcing profit sharing, Worthington announced a no-layoff policy. In a cyclical industry like steel, the no-layoff policy was a real benefit for workers, and no one at the company has ever been laid off because business was slack.[124] If there was insufficient machine work to go around, Bentz recalled, employees would grab paintbrushes and mops and clean the factory.[125]

In turn, Worthington expected workers to give their best efforts. As he instituted paid absences for all employees, McConnell told his crew that if they called in sick and he later discovered they'd gone rabbit hunting, they would be fired because it wasn't fair to others under profit sharing.[126]

And, rather than installing a quality control department, Worthington required each worker to be responsible for quality. Employees were given the power to refuse to ship product if they thought the quality was substandard, a decision traditionally left to management.[127] The result? A product rejection rate that was less than 1 percent in the early 1990s, compared to about 3 percent for other steel processors.[128]

"When I started in business for myself," he told the Newcomen Society in 1980, "I was determined not to have unions. I have no ill feelings toward them; however, I've always believed that management organizes unions, unions do not organize unions. If you run your operation properly and if you are fair, honest and straightforward and keep your people informed, your employees will not want to be represented by an outside party."[129]

A Worthington worker takes a sample from a master coil. The company quickly gained a reputation for quality products.

CHAPTER THREE

TOO BIG FOR ITS NAME

1968–1971

"When I moved to Chicago [in the 1970s], I looked up steel processors in the yellow pages. There were six pages of steel processors and steel service centers. And I thought, 'What is going to differentiate us from every one of these processors here if we're going to grow our business?... What makes us different?'"

— Ralph Roberts, president, Worthington Steel[1]

IN ITS FIRST 12 YEARS, THE Worthington Steel Company enjoyed a rise in sales from $350,000 in its first year to more than $12.5 million in 1967.[2] Behind these numbers was an explosion in profitability that occurred despite tightening competition in metals processing. It was a fractured time in the U.S. steel industry. As the big integrated mills retreated from commodity products, the new minimills, foreign steel manufacturers and independent processors like Worthington carved out slices of the market for themselves.[3] Moreover, the existing service centers began to expand their role into processing.

These service centers were an established link in the supply chain. Traditionally, they acted as distributors that purchased steel from the major producers, warehoused it and then resold it, usually without changing the product. Like Worthington, the service centers benefited from nonunion labor, an intimate relationship with steel producers and the ability to provide specialized, custom service. As the processing market opened up, however, service center owners began to reach out beyond their usual role. In 1968, an enterprising service center could buy a few pieces of equipment (albeit large and costly equipment) and enter into the steel processing business. Many of them did, and as distributors moved into slitting, shearing, drilling, bending or adding coatings, the line between service center and processor began to blur.[4]

Worthington, however, occupied a unique position. It was neither a service center with small capacity processing nor a huge corporation with the demand for large tonnages. It could produce specialized orders with a faster turnaround than the large mills, yet offer better quality and a broader range of techniques, especially the one-pass strip, than service centers. In this sense, Worthington was the first of its kind and created a market niche where none had existed before.

This relative lack of competition showed in the company's financials. Between 1965 and 1968, Worthington doubled net sales from $8.3 million to $16.6 million. Correspondingly, earnings grew from $150,000 to almost $370,000.[5]

Worthington was determined to capitalize on its successes. In the late 1960s, The Worthington Steel Company embarked on a program of expansion and diversification that would transform it into a full-scale leader in the metals-finishing market.

Worthington's first major diversification, which took place in the early 1970s, was into the small-cylinder business. These cylinders were used for a variety of products, including propane fuel.

In need of more cash to fuel growth, Worthington Steel, which later changed its name to Worthington Industries, went public in 1968. A $750 investment in that IPO would have been worth more than $250,000 three decades later.

Worthington Goes Public:
The Capital Years

Expansion, of course, required capital — and with Worthington's capital expenditures steadily rising, officers decided a public offering would be the best way to infuse the company with money. On October 29, 1968, The Worthington Steel Company debuted as a publicly traded company.[6]

At the time of the IPO, officers listed included John H. McConnell, president and director; Merwin Ray, executive vice president and director; Porter Rardin, vice president and director; Charles D. Minor, secretary and director; Clyde V. Tippett, treasurer and director; Ned K. Barthelmas, director; and Don Malenick, vice president, manufacturing.[7]

Naturally, the board was delighted when the offering was immediately oversubscribed. More than 1,200 shareholders purchased 150,000 shares at $7.50 each.[8]

With the new cash, Worthington grew even more rapidly. Sales for 1969 passed $21 million, an increase of 26.8 percent over the previous year.[9] This was the seventh consecutive year in which sales and earnings growth rates were higher than the industry average.[10]

"Yes, it was a very good year!" McConnell told employees in the July 1969 edition of *MetalPhonics*, the company newsletter.[11] He pointed out that the accomplishment had come despite a general decline in the steel industry, as well as "chaotic" working conditions because of plant construction and the installation of new equipment.[12]

That same year, the company installed new 36-inch heavy gauge slitting lines at both plants. These were capable of pulling six cuts at .250 inch thick, a substantial increase over the limit of .187 inch on the old machines.[13] Worthington now had the capacity to cut metal paper-thin to meet even the most demanding specification.[14] The new lines were also automatic, making operations faster and easing some of the physical burden on workers. Production capabilities at Columbus increased by one-third, while the Louisville capacity was almost doubled.[15]

At Columbus, the addition of a third 160,000-pound rolling mill, which could handle coils up to 72 inches in diameter and roll heavy-gauge low carbon steel up to .275 inch in thickness, gave the plant a 30 percent greater capacity in heavy gauges and alloys.[16]

Building Expansion

At the same time, the company kicked off its third major construction spree in five years. New buildings in Columbus added 28,000 square feet, providing needed warehousing and storage space, as well as offices for the growing staff.[17] A similar addition at Louisville added 13,200 square feet.[18]

"With growth," noted Ray in 1969, "comes complexity."[19] Worthington faced the challenge of maintaining its strengths — quality, service and efficiency — on increasingly grander scales. During a three-year period, from 1968 to 1971, the company concentrated on finding ways to maximize all three areas.

The Computer System

At Columbus, the office expansion housed a newly installed computer facility that enhanced both workflow efficiency and customer service. A 1975 article in *Sales Management* made an observation that would seem quaint in later decades: "Computer-based information systems are giving two powerful and vital assists to the marketer's service function: 1) boosting salesmen's productivity by taking over many of the manual chores that eat into critical selling time and 2) strengthening all-important customer relations by triggering more effective responses to customer needs."[20]

Answering a simple customer inquiry, for example, could mean several hours of sifting through shipping and manufacturing records. The extensive system Worthington installed in 1969, though primitive by later standards, revolutionized its business. Seven different inventories were continuously updated in such categories as ferrous and nonferrous raw materials so a complete printout, which previously had taken two days to generate, could be accomplished in a matter of minutes.[21] Daily inventory reports identified the physical specification of each coil of steel in stock, analyzed the cost of material received and shipped, and calculated the average cost of coils on hand. This information eliminated duplicate sales of the same product.[22]

Bob Klein, who was hired in 1967 as a sales trainee, called the computer system a service tool because it allowed the customer to "keep close track of the material he has ordered, which in turn allows him to be more flexible regarding production schedules, sales planning and delivery dates."[23] Klein was an Ohio State alumnus who played halfback under coach Woody Hayes.[24]

To improve response time and efficiency, the Columbus and Louisville plants were furnished with computer systems that tracked the company's inventories, orders and sales.

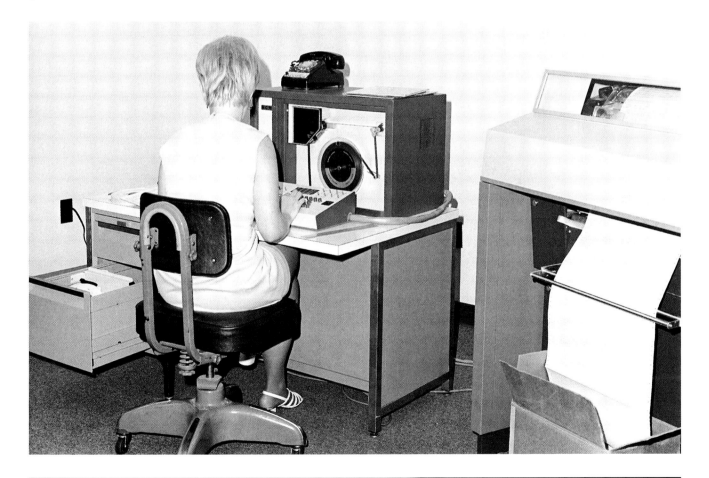

Above: The Testing Laboratory and Quality Control
Department was established in 1967 under the direction
of F.F. "Fritz" Schmidt.

Center: The Testing Laboratory, which was later renamed
Technical Services, was one of the earliest of its kind in the
processing industry and rivaled the service offered by Big Steel.

The Testing Laboratory

Worthington was also determined to build a customer service operation that rivaled anything offered by the bigger mills. The advantage of this was obvious: Small-order customers could turn to Worthington for custom jobs with the same confidence they had in established Big Steel. To this end, the company established the Testing Laboratory and Quality Control Department under the direction of F.F. "Fritz" Schmidt.[25]

The lab, the first of its kind in the processing industry, had a twofold purpose: to maintain quality standards by testing all raw material for type, gauge, hardness and surface quality; and to support the sales staff.[26] The technicians were frequently asked to make recommendations before an order was placed — in other words, to close a sale.

"We look ahead," said Schmidt. "We try to foresee any manufacturing problems that might arise and solve them before production begins."[27]

In metal processing, even tiny differences in composition can be costly in both time and material. The staff of the Testing Lab was comprised of scientists and technicians. In the Lab, tensile testing equipment calculated the maximum load a material could withstand before fracturing and how far it would stretch without breaking. Fracture testing determined the formability characteristics of almost any material.[28] This way, the Lab could determine how a material would react when subjected to a manufacturing process, thus taking the guesswork out of filling customer orders.[29]

Schmidt was soon able to provide specific examples of how the Testing Lab helped customers. After one longstanding customer complained of poor production, Worthington technicians conducted experiments to determine the right hardness and proper steel grade for the application. With better forming and longer die life, production increased about threefold.[30] Another manufacturer was troubled by material failure during a simple forming operation until Lab scientists recommended a change in steel temper.

Below: Scientists and metallurgists at the Testing Lab played a crucial role in establishing Worthington's reputation for technical excellence and helped manufacturing be more efficient.

"Not only did the customer save money by making less scrap," reported Schmidt, "he was able to boost production through a smoother running press operation."[31]

Furthermore, by enhancing the company's reputation for unmatched customer service, the Lab allowed Worthington to command premium prices.[32] For 1970, the first full year of the Lab's operation, Worthington Steel exceeded 98 percent quality performance, giving it a rejection rate of less than 2 percent — much better than the industry average.[33]

By 1971, the technical staff had helped the company expand into new areas of specialization, including spring steel, silicon grades and special grain-controlled products.[34] That same year, the Lab purchased a contact ultrasonic instrument capable of detecting flaws in materials that otherwise could not have been found without actually breaking the material. With this equipment, Worthington could produce high-quality materials with a thickness down to

.01 inch and accuracy approaching .0001 inch from one side.[35]

Forging Knowledge

This unique position in its industry demanded that Worthington develop a unique kind of training program. As a smaller company with high-quality processes, its executives and sales staff were often asked to know many technical areas and to deal more directly with customers and manufacturing than perhaps might happen at a larger company. As the company grew, Worthington incorporated hands-on experience into its formal training. Jack Graf, who joined the company later in the decade, remembered how this management training program worked:

"I started out as a sales trainee working in the plant. You start right on the banding line banding coils of steel to wood skids, and you work your way up the banding line to each piece of equipment. You do that from 7 A.M. until 3 P.M., and then you go in, shower, change your clothes and put on your shirt and tie, and go into the inside sales desk. There, you spend another three hours training. So for the first six months, you basically work from 7 A.M. until about 6 at night."[36]

The Inside Sales Department at Worthington Industries, pictured in the early 1970s. All of these salespeople were trained on the factory floor to learn Worthington's capabilities first-hand.

IN SEARCH OF
RUBBER SOFTENING CREAM...

DURING THE MONTHS THAT NEW MAN–agement hires spent working on the plant floor, they were expected to learn steel processing the hard way — by doing it. This tough orientation served many purposes. Not only did it acquaint a new employee with Worthington's capabilities, it gave workers and management the opportunity to know each other in a personal way.

This built an invaluable sense of esprit de corps as new management found out what it's like to work on the factory floor and the hourly workforce had a chance to meet, and sometimes even trick, the future leaders of their company.

"They'll play little tricks on you," recalled Ike Kelley, Worthington's director of personnel. "They'll send you after things that don't exist, like gauge reducers and edge benders and rubber softening cream and rotary knife sharpeners and coil grabbers. I mean everything sounds like it makes sense."[1]

Kelley, who never did locate the rotary blade sharpener he ventured off to find, remembered how workers once hit the emergency stop button on a piece of machinery while a trainee was looking the other way. The greenhorn, who later became a high-level manager, was sent off on an important mission to locate a "backup roll crank" that was supposedly needed to get the machinery working again.

"They sent him to every mill we had, which isn't a long distance, and when he got to the last one, they said, 'Oh, they took that back to maintenance,'" Kelley said. "He went back there, and they said, 'What are you looking for?' And he told them."[2]

That was when the future executive learned that he had actually been chasing after a wild goose.

"It was part of the way we acclimated our people to the business," Ralph Roberts, future president of the Steel Group, explained, "but more importantly, it created a bond with our people. Over the years, I've really respected that bond because the guys that have trained me down in those slitters and those old rolling mills are now retiring. When I see them, I hear them going, 'You know, I trained that guy.'"[3]

Especially for sales people, this training proved critical. It gave them a solid grounding in what Worthington's capabilities were, meaning they intuitively knew the difference between a good order and one that would be impossible to fill. Ike Kelley, who also began his career at Worthington as a sales trainee, remarked that "We've always had this saying around here: Sales may get the first order, but production gets the rest. If you don't produce what the customer wants, you're not going to get reorders."[37]

After working in the plant, sales trainees often moved to the Testing Laboratory to learn about quality[38] before permanently joining the Inside Sales Department. While the outside salesmen worked with the Testing Lab to gain orders, members of Inside Sales concentrated on filling them. Customers who telephoned Worthington Steel to place reorders, request price quotations or verify delivery dates were connected to Inside Sales. Each of the salesmen was assigned particular customers so that he and his assistants could become familiar with their special requirements.[39]

The 20th Anniversary

Worthington headed into its 20th year in great shape. Despite a depressed U.S. economy in 1970, the company ended the year with an order backlog of more than $3.8 million, and it surpassed the $1 million mark for earnings. It had more than 225 employees and a market reach that extended across 22 states.[40] That year, the plants at Columbus and Louisville shipped more than 131,000 tons of steel to a variety of customers in the automotive, appliance, furniture, communications and office equipment markets. In 1955, by contrast, the company had shipped only 1,000 tons.[41]

The year was also important for other reasons. The Finance and Accounting Department was split into its two functions. Treasurer Clyde Tippett continued in his finance role, while Bob Calentine took over accounting administration in addition to his duties in material management.[42] A few months later, William J. McLaughlin, a graduate of Ohio State University, joined Worthington as vice president of finance, and B.J. Armstrong was promoted to vice president of sales.[43] Also a graduate of Ohio State University, Armstrong had been named to the All Big Ten Football Team in 1962.[44] He had joined Worthington in 1964 and risen through the sales operation. Shortly after his promotion to vice president of sales, he was named general manager of the Louisville plant.

At the same time, the company bid farewell to two of its three original supporters. Margaret Orth and Porter Rardin both retired, each after 15 years of service. Their "loyalty and enthusiastic acceptance of any assignment have contributed immeasurably to the success and growth of Worthington Steel," noted *MetalPhonics* in wishing each a happy retirement.[45]

With the addition of a cold-reduction rolling mill in 1970, business at the Louisville factory boomed. New storage space housed both incoming master coils and completed orders (foreground, with tags) waiting to be shipped.

Branching Out:
Rolling Up New Business

Worthington had grown quickly and was an established steel processor, yet McConnell wasn't satisfied. The steel industry was a tough, unpredictable business subject to wide swings over which no single company had control. McConnell wanted to protect his company against the cyclical nature of the industry by acquiring other businesses in related areas. In June 1971, he found the perfect target in what he has called the "best business deal ever made" and the first diversification for Worthington Steel. This was the purchase of a struggling pressure cylinder business from Columbus-based Lennox Industries.[46]

A family-held corporation, Lennox manufactured heating and cooling systems, but its cylinder operation was losing money. As a supplier to Lennox, Worthington knew it would be a good fit for several reasons. First, the cylinder operation would be a "captive customer" of Worthington steel.[47] Second, a consistent supply of steel and aluminum would help the efficiency and cost strategy of the cylinder operation. Finally, scientists at the Testing Lab could ensure that cylinders met strict U.S. Department of Transportation regulatory requirements, which was a problem for Lennox.[48]

Worthington bought the machinery and equipment associated with Lennox's cylinder manufacturing. At the same time, a group of Lennox employees moved over to Worthington Steel. Among them was a welder named Virgil Winland.

"Cylinders take a real specific talent to build," Winland said. "Probably the biggest difference between the two companies was the work ethic. To survive in Worthington, which was a profit-sharing company, you had to work hard every day. Lennox was a union operation, but Worthington was different because we didn't have quotas; we had the motivation of profit sharing."[49]

The Cylinder Division, founded in the purchase of Lennox Industries, later became active in all phases of cylinder manufacture, including equipment for recycling refrigerant gases, thought to contribute to ozone depletion.

CYLINDER MANUFACTURE... THE PERFECT FIT

WHEN WORTHINGTON BOUGHT Lennox's cylinder business, it bought an operation that complemented its expertise perfectly.

In preparation for cylinder manufacture, coils of flat-rolled steel were pickled to remove surface oxides. The steel was then cut to the desired length. Since most of the steel Worthington bought was open tolerance (meaning the thickness varied throughout the coil), the steel was further cold-reduced to a close tolerance. After cold rolling, it was annealed, or heat treated, making it softer and relieving the stress of cold reduction.[1]

At this point, the steel was ready for blanking — the first step in cylinder manufacturing. It was shipped to the pressure cylinder plant and cut into specific shapes (in this case for various-sized cylinders and their parts).

These shapes were next moved into presses, where they were formed into cylinder halves. Depending on the product, collars and foot rings were welded to the halves, which were then joined by a circumference weld. A valve was added later.

Finished cylinders were typically heat-treated to relieve stress in the steel. This process was controlled closely to give each cylinder specific metallurgical properties. After a multiple-step cleaning process, a two-part polyurethane paint was applied to protect the container from rust. Following heat-induced curing, labels were added and the product was ready for packaging.[2]

Below left: During cylinder manufacture, welders join component parts together into completed units. The process uses processed steel, making it an excellent match with Worthington's operation.

Below right: Once completed, the cylinders were fitted with a collar and valve, and painted. These cylinders are ready to be shipped to customers in a variety of industries.

Lennox continued to fill orders under the name Worthington Cylinders until October, when all operations were moved into a new facility adjacent to a new processing plant that was under construction at Columbus. With the cylinder operation, Worthington gained national marketing opportunities in the refrigerant gas, recreational vehicle and materials handling industries.[50]

"The long-established and successful relationship between our two firms led to a purchase agreement that will aid both companies in achieving long-term growth goals," McConnell announced. "We're very pleased to be able to add a product line that so effectively blends with and complements our present production and marketing activities."[51]

In 1971, the small-cylinder market was in its infancy but poised for rapid growth. Demand for liquefied petroleum gas (LPG) cylinders, originally used in forklifts and recreational vehicles, began to soar with the success of the barbecue gas grill. Likewise, the need for refrigerant cylinders skyrocketed with the popularity of air conditioning.[52]

Worthington Cylinders turned a profit in its first year and later grew into the leading global supplier of low-pressure and high-pressure cylinders. The purchase of Lennox Industries' cylinder business was also the beginning of Worthington's broad, decades-long diversification. In 1971, McConnell signaled his intention to keep diversifying and decided that the annual report would be the last to bear the name Worthington Steel. He split the company into two larger divisions: the Special Products Division to direct the production and marketing of cylinders[53] and the traditional Worthington Steel business. Both were folded under the umbrella of Worthington Industries, a new company name.[54]

Almost immediately, Worthington Industries began setting sales records Worthington Steel had only dreamed of.

John H. McConnell was pleased with Worthington Cylinders' success and vowed to continue diversification. To reflect this strategic shift, the company's name was changed to Worthington Industries in 1971.

Don Malenick, left, and John H. McConnell, right, in the cylinder plant. This new division was immediately successful.

CHAPTER FOUR

STRENGTHENING THE CORE

1972–1977

"It's amazing what Mr. McConnell has done. He's done a lot of capitalization at Worthington when the economy was in the dumper. As it would happen, we'd get our new facility up or our new piece of equipment up and about that time the economy was kind of turning around and off we'd go."

— Ed Ferkany, executive vice president, Worthington Industries[1]

DIVERSIFICATION INTO CYLINders was designed to protect Worthington from swings in the steel industry — never to distract the company from its original business. Fortunately, in the early 1970s, that business was at its peak. The short period between 1972 and 1974 marked the last of the great booms for the old U.S. steel industry. Records were set for production, shipment, sales and profits.[2]

In 1973, at the peak of the boom, the industry was limited only by its own production capacity: Most integrated steel mills were operating at 100 percent and allocating work time to customers. In these conditions, forecasters predicted that the worldwide demand for steel would soar to 900 million tons annually by 1980. The International Iron and Steel Institute announced plans to increase global production capacity by 240 million tons by the end of the decade. This would have raised production potential by nearly one-third.[3]

Naturally, Worthington reaped the rewards from this boom. Sales surged 44 percent from 1971 to 1972, up to $41.6 million, and earnings increased 46 percent to $2.3 million. Also, and largely because of the cylinder operation, the company more than doubled its staff from 258 employees in 1971 to 550 in 1972. In a letter to shareholders, John H. McConnell called 1972 "the most gratifying and dynamic in our 17-year history."[4]

Much of this prosperity was reinvested in the company. In a single year, capital expenditures jumped 826 percent to more than $2.5 million.[5] Worthington broke ground on a new industrial complex located on a 22.7-acre tract near Interstate 270 north of Columbus. Later that year, the pressure cylinder manufacturing, warehousing and office support operations moved into new 82,500-square-foot quarters, and on top of that came the completion of a new Metals Processing Center and a separate Technical Services Laboratory two months later.[6]

Spreading the Cheer

The good fortune was also felt directly by employees. Since its inception in 1966, the profit-sharing plan had disbursed more than $1 million among nonexecutive employees.[7] As a complement to the profit-sharing plan, Worthington also introduced a comprehensive retirement program.

Worthington Steel–Chicago was founded through the acquisition of United Flat Rolled Products in 1972. The plant was heavily modernized after the acquisition and became a leading facility for the company.

In this program, a portion of pretax earnings, in addition to any voluntary contributions, was put into a deferred plan twice a year. After three years, participants became 30 percent vested and earned an additional 10 percent each subsequent year. This benefits program became one of the most comprehensive in the industry.[8]

As the various profit-sharing programs became more complex, McConnell embarked on an educational drive.[9] To communicate how crucial profit sharing was to both workers and the company, Worthington established a series of seminars for groups of 20 to 30 employees. In effect, these were miniature finance and economics lessons. "We start by reviewing our current financial statements with them and giving the sales outlook," explained McConnell, who taught the first round of classes himself.

"Then we take them through a profit and loss statement step by step and show them how a *company makes profit and what expenses have to come out of each sales dollar. We do this because unfortunately most people have great misconceptions about profit. Many people think if you sell a dollar's worth of product, you make a dollar; national surveys show the average conception of corporate profits is 35 percent of sales."[10]*

After demonstrating how small a percentage profit actually was (about a nickel on every dollar, in Worthington's case), McConnell gave lessons on which expense items workers could help control, such as absenteeism, scrap rates, rejection rates, equipment and supplies usage, and so on.

"We might say, for example, 'OK, you can't control the cost of the raw material, but you can lessen how much of it we lose by reducing the scrap rate,'" McConnell said about his program. "We then show them in dollars and cents how much scrap we generated and what effect reducing that number would have on the bottom line.

The Columbus industrial complex, pictured in 1975. From background to foreground: corporate headquarters, the processing plant and the cylinder plant. The bare area in the extreme foreground is now the site of Worthington Machine Technology.

Then we show how much more profit sharing there could be with the lower scrap rate."[11]

The retirement plan proved to be another jewel in the company's employee relations crown. At the end of the decade, the value of the company's contributions exceeded $16 million, and 10 years after that, long-term employees began retiring with as much as $1 million in their accounts.[12]

Although this kind of nest egg was a long ways off for most employees in the early 1970s, and Worthington was still a small company, it was attracting attention for its reputation. In 1973, for example, a recent Ohio State University graduate named Ralph Roberts began looking for a job. To support his family, Roberts had recently bought a gas station while he interviewed at companies like IBM, Spaulding and Worthington. After several interviews with Worthington vice president B.J. Armstrong and others, Roberts was offered a job. "I liked Worthington," Roberts remembered.

"Although I really thought I'd probably go to work for IBM. But the quality of people I'd met at Worthington was different, so I went to my finance counselor at Ohio State, Dr. Cole, and I sat down with him and said, 'I've got these offers. What do you think of these companies?'

"He said to me, 'John McConnell has got a vision and a management style that no one else in this country offers right now. To have faith in the people and to offer profit sharing, that is a new dimension in management. They're a smaller company, they'll give you flexibility to be yourself.' That was probably the reason I came to Worthington."[13]

Buying Power

Worthington was small but wouldn't remain that way, and John H. McConnell continued looking for good acquisition opportunities to expand his steel processing division. In 1972, a second acquisition was announced, and

Worthington completed the purchase of United Flat Rolled Products.

Founded in 1947, United Flat Rolled Products served the Illinois, Wisconsin, western Michigan and northern Indiana areas with slit, cut-to-length and rolled metal products. In 1971, United Flat Rolled Products recorded sales of $7.4 million.[14] After the acquisition, Worthington gained nearly 100 employees and two locations totaling 124,000 square feet adjacent to Chicago's O'Hare International Airport and in East Chicago, Indiana.

Worthington soon sold the Indiana plant and named the remaining facility Worthington Steel–Chicago.[15] The plant was modernized with heavy gauge slitting and cold reduction mill

This cooling tower was part of a sophisticated annealing furnace at Columbus. The equipment was installed at Worthington Steel–Chicago and helped enhance the company's position in the market for cold rolled strip.

equipment.[16] Likewise, the marketing efforts shifted toward the close-tolerance strip business, where competition was limited and profit margins were relatively high. By 1974, strip steel accounted for 39 percent of total shipments at Worthington Steel–Chicago, compared to only 9 percent the previous year.[17]

A year later, Worthington continued its acquisitions with the purchase of the Southeastern Steel Rolling Mills Corporation, a privately owned processing firm with offices in Charlotte, North Carolina, and 24,000 square feet of production space in Rock Hill, South Carolina.[18] Like Chicago, the new Worthington Steel–Rock Hill subsidiary was quickly expanded and modernized, tripling the size of the plant.[19]

Now with processing plants in Columbus, Louisville, Chicago and Rock Hill, Worthington enjoyed a "triangle of support within the largest metal-using market in the nation."[20] In April 1973, the Louisville plant, which had tripled sales in only two years, put the finishing touches on a major addition, thus stretching its market westward to St. Louis and south to Atlanta.[21]

It was a good time to be an expanding steel company. "Basic steel producers are operating at full capacity and are finding it difficult to satisfy total market demand," wrote John H. McConnell in 1973. "The situation is not expected to ease for some time."[22]

In fact, demand was running so far ahead of supply that Roberts, then a new sales trainee, remembered getting the wrong idea of how easy it was to sell steel. "We were getting orders mailed in," he said.

"I was told to open the envelopes and take the orders out and put them in three stacks. First of all, the orders we do on a repetitive basis go in one stack. The orders from customers that we're currently working with go in another stack, and

Steel processing, pictured here in the slitting operation, was a healthy industry in the mid-1970s. One Worthington salesperson remembers customers mailing and phoning more orders in than the company could handle.

Bill Armstrong, the second president of Worthington Industries, succeeded John H. McConnell as president in 1973, during the height of the steel boom. He was president for two years.

orders from people we don't even know go in the third stack. We worked on the first stack and if we had any steel left, we went to the second stack. We pushed the third stack to the back. My first impression of this business was that the orders were just mailed in."[23]

Predicting more growth, Worthington next bought 16 acres adjacent to the Worthington Industrial Park in Columbus.[24] Also, in the existing Columbus facility, Worthington installed three state-of-the-art annealing furnaces with 3,000-ton monthly capacities each, improving the company's position in the cold rolled strip steel market.[25]

A New Team

At the end of the year, a robust Worthington Industries welcomed its second president. Founder John H. McConnell retained his titles of CEO and chairman of the board while ceding the position of president to Bill Armstrong, who served as general manager of the Louisville plant between 1970 and 1973 and was named president of United Flat Rolled Products in 1973.[26] Under his management, the Louisville facility had grown in sales from $7 million to $17 million in just three years.[27]

When Armstrong left for the corporate office, the vacant position of president at United Flat Rolled was filled by Robert Klein. The upper management team was rounded out by Donald Coleman, a new vice president and general manager of Worthington Cylinders, in addition to Don Malenick, executive vice president; W.J. McLaughlin, vice president of finance; and E.H. Newcombe, Jr., president of Southeastern Steel Rolling Mills.

If there was any thread that united many of the company's early employees, it was athletics. Jack Graf, who joined the company in the late 1970s, jokingly remembered that he was one of the few sales trainees at Worthington who was not a former college athlete and that "Whenever I'd walk into a room, here's all these guys that are six foot two and six foot four, and I was five foot ten. It was kind of like walking into the large sequoias out in California."[28]

It turned out that athletes were the perfect personality type for Worthington's concept of teamwork. Worthington was not a superstar company, with employees competing against each other. Rather, it was a team-oriented company. In the early 1970s, a new group of employees joined the company and, like the executives training them, many had played on college teams. Among them was Ed Ferkany, a college football player at Bowling Green and later an assistant football coach under Woody Hayes at Ohio State University. Ike Kelley, who joined as a sales trainee in 1973, had been a college football player and had played for the Philadelphia Eagles. Likewise, Ron Maciejowski, Jack Marsh and Mark Stier, who all joined in the early or mid-

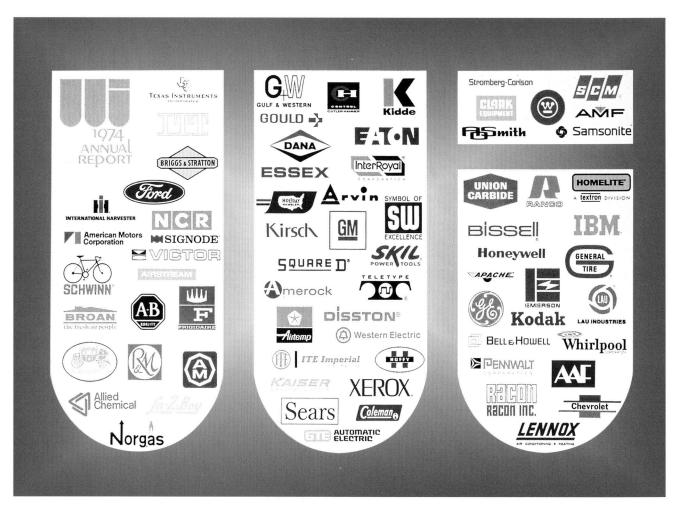

Worthington steel, which had quickly gained a reputation for quality, was used by an impressive array of companies to make more than 6,000 parts for a variety of industries.

1970s, were college-level athletes or members of a coaching staff.

"There are parallels between coaching an athletic team and coaching a business team," said Ferkany, who was 37 when he joined Worthington. "People have to function together. There can't be any barriers in place. Mr. McConnell believes in giving people opportunity. He'll give you the direction he wants you to take the group, and it's your job to carry the ball."[29]

Yet, despite the number of athletes and McConnell's belief in the positive benefits of sports, Worthington did not set out to hire college athletes. "There used to be a joke that you had to

be a former Ohio State player to work here," Marsh said. "It wasn't that. It's like a lot of other jobs. The people you know who have good work ethics are the ones you recommend for the job."[30]

Years later, in fact, McConnell called Ike Kelley, who had become director of personnel, into his office to say, "We're getting a reputation of having a lot of athletes working here. Maybe we ought to put a freeze on the athlete."

Kelley responded, "Mr. Mac, I don't think they should receive preferential treatment because they've played athletics, but I don't think we should penalize them because they've played. If they're Worthington people, and we feel they're Worthington people, shouldn't we hire them?"

McConnell thought about that for a moment, then said, "By God, you're right. Forget I said anything."[31]

Looking back, many people remember 1974 as a fantastic year, and judging from the company's numbers, this was certainly true. Sales that year climbed 30 percent, passing the $37 million mark, and the company continued to post incredible numbers.[32] Over the previous five years, Worthington's annual growth rates in sales, earnings after tax and earnings per share placed the company in the top one-half of 1 percent of all U.S. companies, regardless of industry.[33] Furthermore, Worthington's employees were among the most productive in their industry. Although sales jumped 30 percent in 1974, total employment rose only 11 percent.[34]

Worthington's list of 600 customers read like a who's who among U.S. corporations, including Sears, Roebuck, Honeywell, IBM, Samsonite, Eaton, Xerox, Bissell, Union Carbide, Kodak, Bell & Howell, Chevrolet, General Tire, Schwinn, La-Z-Boy, Briggs & Stratton, Texas Instruments and Whirlpool.[35] These and other companies used Worthington steel to manufacture more than 6,000 different parts and products.[36] Worthington steel appeared in tuning devices for television sets, plated sprockets for bicycles, swivel mechanisms for office chairs, seat channels for automobiles, door hinges for refrigerators, telephone relays and heat treated blades for lawn mowers.[37]

In a letter to shareholders in the 1974 annual report, McConnell and Armstrong wrote that the outlook for 1975 and beyond was excellent:

"We enter the year with an order backlog of $21.2 million.... We foresee a pickup in automotive business and expect strong demand in our other major market areas. We fully expect to exceed our financial objectives of a 20 percent growth in earnings per share and a 20 percent return on shareholders' equity."[38]

The Crisis Coming

Unfortunately, this optimistic future was not to be, and the stream of mailed orders would soon cease. The cause had its roots in a decision made in 1968, when the Lyndon B. Johnson administration, bowing to pressure from congressional representatives of major steel-producing states, agreed with foreign steelmakers to limit the growth of U.S. imports. Under the Voluntary Restraint Agreement (VRA), Japanese and European steel-

makers adhered to yearly quotas for five years, with growth rates capped at 5 percent.[39]

In October 1973, just as the VRA was set to expire, five Arab nations attacked Israel during the Yom Kippur holiday. During the ensuing war, OPEC established an oil embargo against nations friendly to the Israelis, creating a crisis in the United States symbolized by long lines at the gas pump. Inflation rose; consumer spending dropped. As Christopher Hall explains, only a few months after McConnell and Armstrong penned their optimism, the bottom dropped out of the U.S. steel industry.

"The economy, battered by the 1973 oil shock and by adjustment to the end of the Vietnam War, entered a deep recession just at a time when VRAs had been terminated and steel users were frantically trying to build up inventories. Mills went from carefully rationing their customers by 'allocations' through the summer, to layoffs by the end of the year.... As the seriousness of the situation emerged, the expansion plans [at the integrated mills] were quietly shelved again, and the industry slowly began to face up to an era of declining consumption — and the surprisingly rapid decline of the integrated industry."[40]

Foreign steel flooded into the market after the VRAs expired, and Worthington did what it could to protect its segment of the American steel industry. McConnell even refused to buy cheaper foreign steel because he considered it "unpatriotic."[41] To help the struggling Detroit auto manufacturers — Worthington's single biggest market for processed steel — he awarded cash bonuses to employees who bought domestic cars.[42]

For 1975, Worthington's sales increased only 3 percent, a substantial fall from the 30 percent growth rate the company had achieved over the five previous years. Sales for the processed metal division actually fell $800,000, or 1 percent. Likewise, United Flat Rolled Products, because of its location near recession-flattened Chicago, was hit hard with a $4.1 million, or 23 percent, decline.[43]

Despite the hard times, Worthington went ahead with its expansion plans. In 1975, the company spent more than $6.2 million on a variety of projects, including doubling the size of the Columbus processing facility.[44] There were two good reasons to expand during the slump. First, Worthington officers knew it was temporary. Second, the company was still growing, albeit slowly, because of its diversified product mix. Increased business in the pressure cylinder division, for instance, offset the slump in steel processing. For 1975, cylinder sales rose a very healthy 36 percent and contributed to the company's 25 percent boost in pre-tax earnings.[45]

Although the company had fallen short of its goal, its ability to weather tough economic times did not escape notice. Ten years later, *Fortune* magazine would recognize Worthington as one of a few "Corporate Stars that Brightened a Dark Decade."[46]

John P. McConnell Joins Worthington

An inauspicious year for sales, 1975 was notable for two other events. In May, finally finished with its expansion at Columbus, the company moved into a new 30,000-square-foot corpo-

The Columbus processing facility and slitting lines, pictured in the mid-1970s. By this time, the plant featured 206,000 square feet and was Worthington's flagship operation, capable of a wide range of processing techniques, including slitting, cold rolling, roller leveling, edge rolling and annealing.

rate office building. This new building physically incorporated some of the concepts that John H. McConnell espoused to his employees. The headquarters included a full-service barbershop and nice cafeteria. Both served dual purposes. The barbershop was not only convenient and inexpensive, but John H. McConnell believed personal appearance reflected in a person's work. Moreover, the barber soon sat at the center of an informal grapevine. "The barber carried a wealth of information," remarked Bruce Ruhl, who started as a sales trainee later in the decade.[47]

Likewise, the cafeteria was designed to keep employees on the campus during lunch. Instead of spending time in traffic, Worthington employees could fraternize and eat on the premises of the new Worthington Industries Industrial Park.[48]

The other important development that year was a new addition to the employee roster: A second John McConnell joined the staff. John P. McConnell was little more than one year old when his father, John H., founded Worthington Steel in 1955. Growing up, he often accompanied his dad to the Columbus plant on weekends, where he swept floors and collected Coca-Cola bottle caps.[49] Throughout high school, John P. mowed lawns and worked cleanup at Worthington Steel from time to time but wasn't sure if he wanted to follow in his father's footsteps. Scott Jamieson, a childhood friend and teammate at Thomas Worthington High School, later told *Columbus CEO* magazine that, as a boy, John P. "confided that being the son of a well-known businessman wasn't always great."[50]

"The older he got, it became apparent that he felt the pressure of following in his father's footsteps," Jamieson remembered. "When you're trying to follow a legend, it's not easy. It's hard for the son to come in and top what his father has done."[51]

John P. agreed that people had always harbored certain expectations of the son of the founder of Worthington Industries.

"People would say, 'You don't have to worry about anything because your life is already set,'" he remembered of his childhood and teenage years. "It bothered me more back then than it did as I grew older because I came to realize it just wasn't true and that it was being said by people who don't know me or my father or his company."[52]

In later years, both McConnell men sat down with reporter Jeff Phillips to discuss the family nature of the business. Phillips wrote:

"Mr. Mac insists he never pushed his son about future plans, preferring to let the boy forge his own path. The son, on the other hand, says he wasn't sure he wanted a career working for his father. Considering the social and political climate when John P. graduated from high school in 1972, the confusion and rebellion are understandable.

"'Yeah, we went through the "Your hair looks like crap. You look like a girl" period,' recalls John P. jokingly."[53]

But while attending the University of Louisville on a football scholarship, John P. gave Worthington a try. He worked second shift as a machine helper at the Louisville plant, where he helped dig foundations for a new slitter. Soon, he began to look forward to a Worthington future.

Back in Columbus, John H. was pleased. "I had always hoped John wanted to be involved with this company," he later admitted.[54]

A New Year Dawning

Despite the lingering economic recession in 1976, Worthington leaders were already looking forward to an upswing. The depressed demand for processed steel was "a temporary situation and continued the aggressive capacity expansion which has characterized our growth in recent years."[55]

Typically, the company continued to build. Early that year, Worthington completed construction on a huge new 113,000-square-foot steel pickling and processing facility in Monroe, Ohio.[56] The plant broadened the company's processing capabilities to include pickling, the chemical removal of the surface oxide, or scale, that developed on steel during hot rolling. Each of the two pickling lines was capable of processing 60,000-pound coils up to 72 inches wide and three-eighths of an inch thick at an estimated capacity of 600,000 tons a year.[57]

Two heavy-gauge slitting lines also were installed to cut material to width after it was pickled.[58] The pickling facility allowed the company to buy raw material in a less-than-finished state,

Left: Worthington Steel–Baltimore, acquired in 1976 as John J. Greer & Company, quadrupled sales in its first five years. In its sixth year, the company moved into this new facility.

Below: In 1976, Worthington completed construction of a 110,000-square-foot plant in Monroe, Ohio. This plant added pickling lines to Worthington's menu of processing capabilities.

which increased the number of potential suppliers, lowered material cost and ensured continued supply during tight market conditions.[59]

Two months after the pickling plant began operating, and 21 years after opening its doors for business, Worthington surpassed the $100 million sales milestone.[60] Shortly afterward, the cylinder division celebrated its newest customer: DuPont, the largest producer of refrigerant gas in the nation.[61]

In the midst of all this good news, company leaders continued looking for good acquisition targets. In June 1976, one was found in the Northeast, where John J. Greer & Company had carved out a healthy processing and distribution business in Baltimore, with connections into Maryland, Virginia, Delaware, New Jersey, New York and Pennsylvania.[62] After buying Greer & Company, Worthington renamed it Worthington Steel–Baltimore.

Harold "Butch" Dell was plant manager of Greer's Baltimore plant before the acquisition and remembered when the Worthington executive team, including John H. McConnell, Don Malenick, Bob Klein and Bill Armstrong, first came to visit his company. "The first thing we looked at were the people's personalities, and in every case their philosophy was the same as ours," Dell remembered.

"They worked hard, they played hard. They let you make decisions and do your job. It was very easy to be in a relationship with people who were of the same philosophy. I remember the first time I met John H. McConnell, and my

In 1976, Don Malenick became the third president of Worthington Industries, succeeding B.J. Armstrong. Malenick would serve as president of the company for the next 23 years.

impression was that he was a very down-to-earth guy. He wasn't fancy, but he didn't waste any words and obviously tried to present a very fair picture to both sides."[63]

A Third President

Later that year, one of the men who helped arrange the Greer acquisition announced he was leaving. B.J. Armstrong, after two years as president of Worthington, left the company. He was succeeded in his position by long-time employee Don Malenick. Malenick's promotion to president and chief operating officer was announced on November 13, 1976.[64]

Malenick's first couple of months in office were good ones. The national economy was indeed improving, and sales in 1977 rose 44 percent to $148.6 million. Almost $10 million came from the new Baltimore and Monroe facilities alone, while metal processing sales increased 43 percent to $127.7 million and pressure cylinder sales rose 53 percent to $20.9 million.[65]

This growth was rewarded in June 1977, when Worthington was included on *Fortune* magazine's list of "The Second 500 Largest Industrial Corporations." The listing was impressive, but the numbers behind it were amazing for a company of Worthington's size and history. Worthington's 23.8 percent return on year-end shareholders' equity ranked 58th in the country. Its 31.25 percent growth rate on 10-year earnings ranked 21st. And its total return to investors for 1976 ranked an astonishing seventh in the United States.

"We believe," wrote John H. McConnell, "we are in the best position ever."[66]

This electric arc furnace is at Buckeye, a 1980 acquisition. The arc furnace technology rapidly replaced the open hearth.

CHAPTER FIVE

THERE IS NO RUST IN COLUMBUS

1978–1983

"I think ethics and honesty are the key to business. I think you can ask anybody around this country, and they will say that Worthington Industries, from day one, through all the turmoil of the seventies and eighties, has never lost its ethical values."

— John Christie, president and COO, Worthington Industries[1]

WORTHINGTON MAY HAVE been in its best position ever, but the rest of the economy was still in trouble. The effects of the recession in the early 1970s were replaced by other unsettling factors heading into the 1980s. Foreign competition, especially, took its toll on the American steel industry as overseas companies revolutionized their approach to manufacturing and inventories. At the same time, Big Labor exerted ever more power over U.S. corporations, which themselves were later accused of lethargy.

In January 1980, the Federal Reserve Board released distressing figures that reflected what was happening across the landscape of American business. Production had risen a weak 0.3 percent from the previous year, the most sluggish performance since the 1974 recession.[2] Business inventories grew 0.7 percent during November 1979, as sales failed to keep pace.[3] Mortgage rates, meanwhile, stood in the double digits, and inflation often reached between 7 percent and 9 percent.[4]

The "malaise," as President Jimmy Carter called it, didn't touch just American business. Americans had been watching the hostage situation unfold in Tehran for 444 terrifying days, and the Cold War threat from the Soviet Union figured prominently in movies and television. From all indications, it seemed as if the 1980s wouldn't be much of an improvement over the decade just finished.

"If you disliked the last half of the 1970s, you are going to hate the first half of the 1980s," wrote Professor Lester Thurow of MIT in the January 27 issue of the *Boston Globe*. "More inflation, higher unemployment, a falling dollar, low growth, skyrocketing energy prices — everything is going to get worse."[5]

During the month of January alone, close to 191,000 autoworkers lost their jobs.[6] U.S. car manufacturers, beleaguered by gasoline shortages, rising labor and materials costs, and the popularity of imported cars, suffered a decline of 20 percent in sales from the previous year, and no improvement was in sight.[7]

The steel industry, however, appeared to be holding its own for the time being. In 1979, American steel companies shipped more than 100 million tons for the first time since 1974.[8] But it was a false sense of prosperity. Unbeknownst to them, steelmakers faced "the start of a slide into the worst trough of the industry's history."[9] In 1980, shipments dropped to 83.8 million tons, rose slightly in 1981 to 88.5 million tons, then plunged to 61.6 million tons in 1982. It was the

---

In June 1983, Worthington debuted on the *Fortune* 500 list of largest industrial companies in terms of revenue. For the previous thirteen years, the company's return on equity was 23.9 percent.

lowest domestic steel output since the 1930s.[10] In total, the Big Steel companies lost $3.3 billion, or 11 percent of their total value.[11]

The sagging domestic industry was mirrored by a boom in imported steel, prompting industry leaders to complain that Japanese and European steelmakers were dumping cheap imports into the U.S. market. More than 18 million tons of foreign steel were shipped to the United States in 1979.[12] Within a year, imports captured more than 16 percent of the raw steel market.[13]

The U.S. steel industry had been caught off guard. American steel was vulnerable as the big integrated mills lost ground to minimills, which — through a combination of specialization and simplified production — could reach economies of scale faster than the integrated plants.[14] The minimills already had usurped the market for small-diameter products. They next began to diversify into more sophisticated products such as wire rods, higher quality bars and medium-sized structural shapes.[15] By 1980, the minimills had carved out 12 percent of the country's raw steel production, up from just 5 percent a decade earlier.[16]

Worthington's Star Among Stars

In 1980, Worthington Industries celebrated its silver anniversary as one of *Fortune* magazine's top 1,000 industrial corporations, ranking 630th on the basis of sales.[17] In total return to investors for the 10-year period, the company ranked number one. Despite several recent acquisitions, more than half its business still came from specialty steel processing, and the auto industry remained a dominant customer: General Motors alone accounted for about 20 percent of steel sales.[18] Naturally, it was only a matter of time until Worthington felt the effects of the troubled auto industry and, in the summer of 1980, John H. McConnell wrote to shareholders:

> *"The steel processing portion of our business was adversely impacted by the sharp downturn in automobile production which began last fall. Months later, as other segments of the economy started to slow down, such as the appliance industry, the rate of incoming orders continued to drop."[19]*

McConnell had carefully qualified an otherwise unqualified success. Worthington Industries was performing profitably through one of the worst steel crises in U.S. history, making it a "star of stars," according to *Fortune*.[20] In 1985, the magazine featured Worthington among the seven "most shrewdly managed organizations ever to make a buck — actually, lots of bucks — from doggy businesses."[21]

The magazine summed up the Worthington formula for success: "To stay alive in a declining industry, companies must avoid battling for market share. They also have to control costs, keep customers coming back with flawless service and improved products, and maintain employee morale."[22]

The Acquisition Strategy: ACT

Although processed steel sales slumped 10 percent in 1980, Worthington stayed profitable partly through diversification.[23] The company had been steadily buying businesses that expanded either its geographic reach in steel processing or its product line and had proved to itself the value of a good buy. Worthington Cylinders was the model for further corporate expansion, company officers noted:

"The pressure cylinder operations, purchased in 1971, quickly began to benefit from the Worthington method of conducting business. We brought to this fledgling situation not only skill and experience in metal working, but our uniquely successful employee incentive programs and sales and marketing expertise. Through the years we have expanded product line and extended market coverage to the point where we are now the leading supplier of refrigerant and LPG cylinders to a variety of growing industries.

"Perhaps most notably, we established with this first acquisition the parameters by which later ones have been made: the businesses we acquire should relate to our current operations, from a manufactur-

In 1977, Worthington acquired Advanced Coating Technology, Inc., a manufacturer of coated glass. The glass was strong enough to be used as an architectural element and was popular with builders.

ing, marketing or technical standpoint; they should show great promise for growth and profitability; and should be involved in the more sophisticated segments of basic industry."[24]

Between 1977 and 1980, Worthington grew substantially by continuing to follow this rough outline. In 1977, the company provided start-up financing to Advanced Coating Technology, Inc., (ACT) a producer of high-quality metallic coated glass.[25] Advanced Coating Technology operated out of a temporary office, lab and pilot facility in Columbus, until construction was completed on a 58,000-square-foot manufacturing plant in Franklin, Tennessee, 20 miles south of Nashville.[26] ACT grew quickly, increasing its number of employees from 70 to 125 in just one year.[27] In June 1979 it became a wholly owned subsidiary of Worthington.[28]

The ACT acquisition was an example of Worthington's ability to capitalize, even briefly, on emerging technologies. High performance coated glass was a darling of builders and consumers in the 1970s, in part because of its energy-saving capacity. Proper use could reduce heating and cooling requirements for certain types of structures by as much as 50 percent.[29] Designers also liked the product because of its aesthetic qualities:

"Virtually immune to the elements, glass allows the architect to control, manipulate and ultimately incorporate light itself as an integral element in the design. Protecting without isolating, glass provides the architect with the opportunity to fuse strength and beauty, combined properties not found in any other construction material."[30]

Worthington's position in the coated glass industry was similar to its role in the steel business, where it purchased a readily available commodity, added value and sold it to the end-user on a customer-order basis. Advanced Coating Technology acquired float glass — the major raw material used to make coated glass — from primary suppliers such as Ford and PPG. ACT applied the reflective coating using its own patented technology, then either sold it in that form or further processed it, for example making it into insulated twin pane units.

The Timbers III in New Orleans, Louisiana. The all-glass facade, supplied by ACT, was energy efficient and attractive. ACT, although successful for a time, was later sold when reflective glass fell out of favor.

Headquartered in Ashland, Ohio, U-Brand Corporation was known for its do-it-yourself brand of pipe fittings, sold nationwide at hardware and home improvement retail locations.

U-Brand Corporation

In March 1978, Worthington turned to another kind of company, one with national presence and an established market share. U-Brand Corporation, headquartered in Ashland, Ohio, a small college town 80 miles north of Columbus, was one of the country's largest manufacturers of malleable cast iron, steel and plastic pipe fittings, as well as pipe nipples and cut lengths.[31] It was founded in 1918 as The Union Malleable Manufacturing Company and had changed names about the same time Worthington Steel became Worthington Industries.[32]

U-Brand, which became a wholly owned subsidiary of Worthington, maintained a foundry and machine shop in Ashland, a plastics plant in Upper Sandusky near Cleveland and a nipple plant located in Puerto Rico. Nationwide distribution was handled from eight warehouses.

One of the first manufacturers of malleable iron pipe fittings to enter the plastics field, U-Brand sold fittings to the plumbing, hardware and industrial markets. It had captured a sizable share of the growing wholesale hardware and "do-it-yourself" home-center market.[33]

Capital Die, Tool and Machine Company

In February 1980, Worthington entered the tool and die making business with the purchase of a long-time supplier, the struggling Capital Die, Tool and Machine Company of Columbus.[34] With more than 80 years' experience, Capital built machines for the heating and cooling industry as well as products such as bottle-filling machines for distilled water; bag-making machines for the packaging of soft drinks, ketchup and wine; and machines used to install vent ducts beneath dashboards.

In its first five years as a Worthington company, Capital Die increased sales by 300 percent and established a base of 100 customers for die servicing and building in the Columbus area alone.[35] Other Worthington divisions benefited from the presence of a machine shop. Capital manufactured test chambers and refrigerant valves for the cylinder division, saving the company $480,000 every year.[36]

That same year, Worthington purchased the properties and assets of I.H. Schlezinger, a processor of recyclable metals for sale to various foundry and steel mill operations in Ohio and surrounding states.[37]

Buckeye

As the list of acquisitions grew, Worthington became more comfortable as a buyer and began pursuing a larger company. In May 1980, the company announced its largest acquisition to date: Buckeye International, Inc., a major manufacturer of steel castings and precision parts. It operated several locations under two divisions, Buckeye Steel Castings and Buckeye Custom Products.[38]

Since its founding in 1880, Buckeye Steel Castings had become a leader in high quality cast steel products ranging in size from 100 pounds to 30 tons.[39] The company originally operated as a cast iron producer, turning to steel production in the late 1890s. When a new automatic coupler for railcars came into use in the early 1900s, Buckeye's long association with the railcar industry began.

Around that time, S.P. Bush, grandfather of former President George Bush, joined Buckeye, serving as president from 1908 through 1927.[40]

Having been in business for a full century, Buckeye was entrenched in tradition and unused to the Worthington way of doing business. On an early plant visit, recalled Bruce Ruhl, who worked in investor relations during the acquisition, a Buckeye line employee approached John H. McConnell. Ruhl recounted the story:

Below and opposite: Buckeye, acquired in 1980, ran one of the largest and most technically modern foundries in the nation. Molten steel was poured into molds to make castings for the railroad, mass transit, oil and gas exploration, defense, and coal mining industries.

"He said, 'Listen, I just want to thank you for being here today. I've been here for 11 years and I've never seen our former president or our chairman walk through our plant, and here you guys, on the first day, here you are.'"[41]

Yet this gesture wasn't enough to erase the differences between the two companies. Buckeye operated heavily unionized shops saturated with the kind of rules and regulations McConnell had deliberately kept out of his company. Ike Kelley, who became group manager of personnel in 1982, then director of personnel in 1985, remembered that Buckeye's multitiered structure was at odds with the more entrepreneurial Worthington.

"They had a manual at one time that literally explained everything you should do when you hired a new employee, from getting up out of your seat and going to the door and shaking hands with this individual to welcoming him to the company. You know: common sense. But they had all that stuff laid out. We kind of took that and said, 'Guys, use your heads,' and pushed that to the side and tried to kind of 'Worthington-ize' it a little bit."[42]

Operating one of the largest single-site steel foundries in the United States, Buckeye produced the railcar industry's broadest and most diversified line of components, including castings.[43] In acquiring Buckeye, Worthington was banking on increased business in the railroad industry, as McConnell hoped in the 1981 annual report.

"The rapid increase in fuel costs and the need to conserve has created renewed interest in the railroads. The average fuel cost of shipping freight by rail is approximately one-fourth the cost of moving it by truck. Road congestion and deterioration, air pollution and labor costs per ton-mile add further impetus to the shift to rail transportation. The need to expand and upgrade freight car fleets has caused increasing demand for castings in recent years. While there will be fluctuation in customer order rates due to changing economic conditions and financing costs, this market is expected to boom in the 1980s."[44]

Steel castings were also vital to the mass transit, oil and gas exploration, defense, and coal mining industries. McConnell also predicted the country would soon turn to its vast reserves of coal as a means of reducing dependence on imported oil. This would benefit Buckeye in two ways: first, by expanding the number of casting orders for train coal cars; and second, by accelerating the need for surface mining equipment, draglines, earth movers and heavy off-highway trucks.

However, Worthington was almost immediately forced to slash prices due to sharp downturns in the railroad freight car and heavy industrial equipment markets.[45] In 1981, some of this lost business was replaced when the company won multimillion dollar contracts to make undercarriages for mass transit subway and commuter trains in New York City, New Jersey, Philadelphia and Long Island.[46]

Buckeye Custom Products, Buckeye's other division, had plants in Salem, Mentor, Mason and Upper Sandusky, Ohio. Its sophisticated range of plastic processing and metal machining capabilities served automotive and truck manufacturers as well as the appliance industry.

Shortly after the Buckeye acquisition, the custom products and castings divisions were split and formed two new operating units in Worthington, bringing the corporate total to four (steel processing, cylinders, castings and custom products). Ed Ferkany was named president of the newly acquired Custom Products Division "even though I had never seen an injection molding machine in my life and I'd never been to any of the plants."

"But the current management wasn't working out and, in John's infamous way, he said, 'It's our people anyway. Just go in there and figure out what you need to do.' I went into the plastics group and found out we did have some very good people who wanted to be Worthingtonized. Well, we weren't making any money, so we took some drastic steps and kind of started over from scratch."[47]

Twenty Years of Breaking Records

In 1981, one year after buying Buckeye, Worthington achieved record sales for the 20th consecutive year. Sales of $428.1 million represented a 49 percent increase over the previous year. This huge increase was driven by excellent sales for pressure cylinders and U-Brand pipe fittings, an increase in steel processing orders, and Buckeye.[48]

That same year, Worthington spent a record $20.9 million on capital expenditures.[49] A major portion of this investment was used to upgrade metal processing equipment or replace it. As Robert Borel, a former Eastman Kodak engineer who joined the company in 1974, explained:

"We never bought new equipment for the first five years I was with the company. We just didn't do it. We bought used equipment, and we rebuilt it, refurbished it, put new parts on it, controls or

what have you, and we were very effective in using a very low asset base to grow the company with. Now as all that equipment dried up for various reasons, it either went overseas to countries that were just developing their industry, or it just plain wore out."[50]

A new, state-of-the-art cylinder manufacturing and steel processing facility went on line in Claremore, Oklahoma, increasing the company's

The blank-feeding line of the cylinder operation at Claremore, Oklahoma. This facility increased Worthington's production capacity by 50 percent in the refrigerant cylinder business.

production capacity by 50 percent in the refrigerant cylinder business.[51]

At Columbus, annealing capacity was doubled. There, the company also installed the nation's most modern three-stand tandem mill for cold reduction of heavy-gauge, high-carbon steel.[52] In order to compete with more energy-efficient Japanese cars, Detroit automakers had realized they needed to dramatically downsize their vehicles. The tandem mill, with its cold reduction capabilities, allowed Worthington to provide very light-gauge, high-strength materials, something few other processors could offer, and thickness that met the most precise specifications. The result was a more refined product, and thus a higher-margin product line.[53]

A new three-stand tandem mill at Columbus used computer technology to control machine speed and steel coil tension and thickness in order to produce superior product.

The State of the Industry, 1985

By the middle of the decade, the American steel industry was not doing well. In his history of the steel industry, *And the Wolf Finally Came*, John Hoerr writes:

"The collapse of the American steel industry represents one of the great industrial failures of modern times. It is not the sole instance of a once-prominent industry caught in a technological revolution or a sudden shift in comparative advantage from one region to another. Had the industry been blessed with the most astute of leaders — and it was not — even that management could not have maneuvered the industry fully out of unstoppable economic forces of the kind that killed the horse-drawn carriage or moved the textile industry from New England to the South. However, the toppling of American steel as the premier metal maker for the West produced consequences far vaster than most industrial fade-outs, in terms of plants shut down, workers dislocated and entire regions thrown into economic decline."[54]

The 1980s were a time of blight for the Northeast and Great Lakes states. Once-mighty manufacturing cities like Detroit, Chicago, Pittsburgh, Cleveland and Akron were severely affected by the recession. From 1980 to 1985, inflation made foreign steel irresistibly cheap. Imports rose to 26.4 percent of consumption in 1985.[55] The situation was aggravated by an overvalued dollar, which drove up the market share of imported automobiles. Integrated mills lost $12 billion during the decade, offset by only $5 billion in profits.[56] Plants operated at less than half capacity.[57] Between 1974 and 1980, Big Steel had already downsized its union workforce by nearly 15 percent; now the industry had little choice but to close idle capacity and lay off as many workers as possible to stave off bankruptcy.[58] Seventy-five percent of all steel workers in America — more than 320,000 people — lost their jobs.[59]

Although perhaps the most visible symbol of ruin, the steel industry was not alone. Coal mines, potteries, tire factories and automobile plants throughout Pennsylvania, Ohio, West

Virginia and Michigan cut workers or shut down altogether. Collectively called the "Rust Belt," the entire region suffered as jobs went south to Houston and unemployment rates skyrocketed into the mid and high teens.[60]

In 1986, with the Rust Belt still rusting, *Fortune* magazine sent a reporter to Ohio to study what it called the "Columbus Effect." Amid the decay of Cleveland to the north, Pittsburgh to the east, and Steubenville and Wheeling to the south sat the city of Columbus, ripe with prosperity. Of the 1,700 corporations tracked by the Value Line Investment Survey, 12 were headquartered in or near the city, including Wendy's International (the hamburger chain), The Limited clothing stores, Bob Evans Farms restaurants, ChemLawn, BancOne and Worthington Industries.[61]

As the home of a major academic institution, Ohio State University, and surrounded by fertile farmland just outside the city limits, Columbus actually benefited from the absence of a single dominant industry, such as rubber had been for Akron or car manufacturing for Detroit.

John Christie, then president of the Chamber of Commerce and a future president and COO of Worthington Industries, attributed the city's success "largely to Columbus's boomtown atmosphere, which presumably fosters an upbeat mentality in the boardroom."[62] *Fortune* could find no other reason for the city's good fortune beyond its sparkling clean streets and a workforce "built up by migration over the decades from the farms of Ohio and the hills and mines of Appalachia" that was "blessed with what employers invariably call the 'work ethic.'"[63]

Columbus's position as a calm island in the storm paralleled Worthington's own success. In 1982, one of the worst years for the steel industry as a whole, every division at Worthington not only turned a profit but increased market share.[64]

In a 1986 speech, business author Tom Peters used Worthington as an example for other companies. Peters blamed the dire situation in domestic manufacturing on three decades of executive complacency, something Worthington could never be accused of. Instead, John H. McConnell remained so involved that he foresook a traditional emblem of executive status: the corner office. When Dale Brinkman joined the company in 1982 as general counsel, he found himself sitting in one of the nicest offices at the Columbus headquarters.

"I knew Worthington had a great reputation," Brinkman said.

"But I was kind of shocked, and very happy of course, to be in the corner office. I asked, 'Why isn't Mr. McConnell on this side of the building?' You've got the lake on one side and the helipad, and you look over this really nice park setting. But he walked in and said, 'This isn't the office I want. I want to see my plant.' I learned that was part of the Worthington way. This company is not about the trappings of the big offices. People worked, and they were all part of the team."[65]

Peters pointed out that other companies in Worthington's industry had gone in the opposite direction. Although "you had to work pretty hard to screw up a major American corporation" between the years 1946 and 1973,[66] Peters said the American steel industry had gorged on growth and let service and quality drop by the wayside.

In contrast, Peters said, the winners of the 1980s would be small, flat (with few layers of management), specialized, innovative and niche-oriented institutions.[67]

"Worthington people scour their customers' operations looking for opportunities to solicit profitable projects of any size. No order is too small. Plant managers spend up to 25 percent of their time in the field, and salespeople and metallurgists discuss more efficient and cost-effective products with customers regularly.

"Take Worthington's recent work for General Motors. By modifying the seat-adjustment track in GM cars, Worthington cut costs by $25 a ton — a savings of 12.5 percent. When Union Fork & Hoe Company could not make its rakes at a competitive price, Worthington made adjustments in the steel components that resulted in lower immediate sales for Worthington — but it helped Union compete and made Worthington a friend for life."[68]

Peters praised Worthington for being well structured to thrive amid the very conditions that collapsed the traditional, top-heavy, integrated steel mills. The company's leanness made it especially attractive for customers who were struggling to manage their inventories. Typically, Worthington filled orders for automakers within two weeks, at least one month faster than most of its competition.[69]

As Peters had pointed out, nearly three decades of providing superior quality and service had created an intensely loyal customer base. "You develop a very strong relationship with your customers, especially as Worthington expects it to be," said Jack Marsh. "We hope to be more than just a group of steel salesmen out there selling steel. There are people within just about every organization that we sell to that we know from top to bottom, and even when there are changes, we continue to be in touch with not only the person that takes their place but that person, if he stays within the organization."[70]

Productivity within the plants was an equally important element of Worthington's success. Writing for *Forbes* in 1981, William Baldwin noted that Worthington's culture made for extremely high productivity.

"Absentee rates at Worthington's profit-sharing operations are 2 percent, compared with 5 percent in its union shops; Worthington claims its reject rate is 1 percent, compared with 3 percent and 4 percent for the industry. Tons moved per man hour is about a third higher than that for the average steel service center specializing in flat-rolled steel. This in spite of the fact that Worthington is usually doing more to the steel — annealing, cold rolling, pickling — than its competition."[71]

During slow times caused by the recession, Worthington managers had the luxury of reassigning nonunion workers to meet the company's shifting needs. In 1980, some steel workers poured concrete for the installation of the tandem mill while others were moved to the busy cylinder factory.[72] According to *Forbes*, "At Worthington, two men run a slitter; at unionized competitors there are three or more on the larger machines. Perhaps the greatest effect of Worthington's unusual compensation is the one that is hardest to quantify: the stake that profit sharing gives workers in their employer's success."[73]

In the second half of 1983 the general economy began to strengthen, and the automobile and consumer durable goods markets improved. After weathering the lean years with small increases in net sales — 2 percent in 1982 and 3 percent in 1983 — Worthington began a period of fast growth that was all the more impressive because of the continuing ill health in the steel industry.[74] In June 1983, the company broke into the *Fortune* 500 for the first time, ranking 486th on the basis of $437.6 million in sales.[75]

Fortune also included Worthington on an elite list of 13 companies that had provided shareholders with the best return on investment for the troubled years 1974 to 1983. While the median return for *Fortune* 500 companies was 13.2 percent during that period, the magazine conferred "stardom" on companies that averaged at least a 20 percent return and never sank below 15 percent. This was "an extraordinarily high standard ... analogous to a savings account that annually earns the holder 20 percent interest."[76]

Fortune seemed as surprised as anyone to find a steel processor in the number-seven spot. Steel, the article noted, was an industry "normally thought to be ruled by unrewarding commodity economics."[77]

Three factors explained Worthington's success: It had established itself in a special niche for high-margin steel in its market; it produced such a high-quality product that it could charge premium prices; and its management, under the direction of John H. McConnell, had remained both stable and innovative.[78]

During a 10-year period when most stocks malingered in a "painful hangover," Worthington's average return on equity was 23.9 percent, enough to meet the company's stated long-term goal to provide a minimum 20 percent return for shareholders annually.[79] The figure placed Worthington among such powerhouses as Dow Jones (number two with 26.3 percent) and Kellogg (number five with 24.8 percent).

Fortune described the performance as "heroic."[80]

In 1985, Worthington Industries held a company picnic to celebrate its 30th anniversary. President Don Malenick and Chairman, CEO and founder John H. McConnell are in the foreground (left and right respectively).

CHAPTER SIX

GROWING BIGGER, GROWING STRONGER

1984–1987

"We can sell you hot roll. We can sell you cold roll. We can sell you cold roll strip. We can sell you high carbon cold roll strip. We can slit it. We can cut it to length. We can blank it. We can coat it. We can galvanize it. We can nickel plate it. We can electro zinc it.... What do you want?"

— Ed Ferkany, executive vice president, Worthington Industries[1]

B Y THE MID-1980s, THE U.S. economy was in a solid rebound. In January 1984, production levels rose 1.1 percent, the 14th consecutive monthly gain since the recovery began.[2] Inflation had practically disappeared as a serious economic concern, and jobs were being created at a rapid pace.[3] Detroit auto makers sold nearly 6.8 million cars in 1983, their best performance since 1979 and a sharp turnaround from 1982, when sales had hit a 20-year low.[4]

Although one might assume the steel industry would have benefited from the general upturn, the opposite was true. U.S. monetary policy, designed to control inflation by maintaining high interest rates, drove up the value of the dollar, prompting some analysts to warn that the dollar was too strong.[5] According to author Roger Ahlbrandt in *The Renaissance of American Steel*:

"It was devastating for U.S. steel producers. Buyers of steel in the United States could purchase foreign steel with the same strong dollars that made hotels and meals cheap for traveling Americans. Foreign steel producers were attracted to the American market as never before.... By 1984–85 they were supplying one out of every four tons of steel being purchased in this country. These imports flowed into the United States to fill

the demands of steel-consuming industries — such as autos, construction, appliance and heavy equipment — for cheaper steel and, in some applications, for higher-quality steel. As early as 1982, import levels approached 20 percent of the U.S. market, and worse was yet to come."[6]

By 1984, "worse" had arrived. That year, foreign steel accounted for 26 percent of the U.S. market, and operating losses for steelmakers averaged $10 per ton.[7] In January 1985, *Forbes*' description of the industry's decline read almost like a dirge:

"The Forbes Yardsticks for metals tell a sorry tale: 17 of the 38 companies in the group ran deficits, 16 others were unable to match or beat their five-year return on equity averages in the past 12 months, and only five improved on their five-year profitability figures. Of the 42 industries that were tracked by Forbes, metals ranked 37th in profitability."[8]

Throughout the hard years in the 1980s, when the domestic steel industry almost collapsed, Worthington Cylinders continued to post strong numbers because of new products, like this Balloon Time helium tank, and geographic expansion.

Of the companies *Forbes* studied, however, Worthington Industries ranked first in all three categories: profitability, growth and earnings per share. The company's 27.7 percent five-year average return on equity in 1984 easily outpaced runner-up Nucor, the star of the minimills, which posted a 24.4 percent return.[9] Industry-wide, the average median return on equity was less than 8 percent.[10]

Furthermore, Worthington sales posted an 18.8 percent five-year average increase; Nucor, again second, stood at 10 percent.[11] Finally, Worthington was the only metals company with a positive five-year average return on earnings per share, with a robust 43.7 percent return for the previous five years.[12]

"The best-performing companies tend to be smaller, specialized outfits," observed *Forbes*. "Profit-leader Worthington Industries ... boasts markets in processed steel for things like component parts in consumer appliances and auto disk-braking systems."[13]

Compared to giant mills like U.S. Steel and LTV, Worthington was indeed small and specialized. Yet within the niche processing market, the company was a powerhouse, operating 20 facilities and a network of distribution centers throughout the United States and in Puerto Rico.[14] As the nation's premier metal processor, Worthington was the 475th largest industrial corporation in the United States.[15] "They really led the way," remarked David Hoag, chairman of LTV at the time.

"They opened up a new level of distribution in the steel business, and they did a lot of things that the mills had done before and gotten out of for whatever reasons. They were the pioneer at this new level of distribution between the service center and the mills."[16]

Yet operating at this "new level" exacted a cost from Worthington. While the company kept its open-door policy, a certain amount of intimacy had to be sacrificed for prosperity. Chairman John H. McConnell and president Don Malenick sent their holiday greetings through the company newsletter: "It doesn't seem so very long ago when we were able to personally visit with each of you to wish you a happy holiday season. However, as we have grown it has become increasingly difficult to see you when we would like."[17]

With the ability to pickle, anneal, slit, coat, cut-to-length and edge roll, Worthington could do virtually anything to prepare steel for customer use. According to Malenick, Worthington offered the most comprehensive service in the processing industry:

"Total overall services are 17 or 18. We probably do 15 of the processes, whether it's rolling, slitting, annealing, cut-to-length, coating, painting, hot dip, nickel plating, or a combination of things. We are definitely number one in the U.S. as far as numbers of different processes we do in the steel industry."[18]

Worthington was more cost effective on custom orders, responding to short lead times and maintaining a quality acceptance rate of 99 percent.[19] The rejection rate for the industry as a whole averaged around 4 percent.[20]

This enormously successful steel operation, which still accounted for the vast majority of Worthington's sales, was run from eight plants, each marketing to a different part of the United States.[21] Facilities in Columbus and Monroe, Ohio, and Chicago sold to the Midwest. Plants in Louisville, Kentucky, and Rock Hill, South Carolina, marketed to customers in the South and Southeast; while plants in Baltimore, Maryland, and Malvern, Pennsylvania, concentrated on servicing customers in the mid-Atlantic and Northeast regions. A state-of-the-art processing and cylinder manufacturing center in Claremore, Oklahoma, provided Worthington with a gateway to the West. The steel processed in these facilities was used to make more than 7,000 different parts for more than 1,300 industrial customers.[22]

Outside Processing

Steel processing was Worthington's largest division, but the company remained active on a variety of fronts. Its four other divisions each had healthy shares of their markets — custom products (14 percent); pipe fittings (11 percent); pressure cylinders (9 percent); and cast steel (9 percent).

Above: A robot welds the collar on a Worthington cylinder. In the mid-1980s, cylinder manufacture was enhanced with new equipment. The division soon earned a 99 percent customer acceptance rate.

Right: Worthington Custom Products, which included the plastic molding operation, produced parts for hundreds of consumer products throughout the 1980s, including this Lawn-Boy lawnmower. Inset: Custom Products also made precision metal parts.

In custom products, Buckeye produced plastics in three plants and operated a metal machining plant. All together, these four Buckeye plants set records in 1984 for both revenue and earnings, which increased 147 percent over the previous year.[23]

Some of Buckeye's strength in plastics was based on the rejuvenated auto industry. The company manufactured a variety of injection-molded plastics, in addition to precision metal components for power steering, transmission and other mechanical systems. These complementary capabilities in plastics and metals allowed Buckeye to produce completed subassemblies for items such as automobile dashboards and microwave ovens.

In the relatively new pipe fittings business, U-Brand contributed about 11 percent of total sales. U-Brand's 16 distinct product lines consisted of more than 3,400 different items, the most com-prehensive in its industry.[24] Customers were attracted by a unique purchasing method, the Quantity-Unit-Buying program, which allowed them to obtain truck-load-quantity discounts on a mixture of different items.[25]

In 1984, Worthington provided U-Brand with two new tools to broaden its market. First was the acquisition of the Dart Union product line, the leading iron pipe union, which was used to couple pipes or pipes and fittings.[26] Second, Worthington installed a new vertical channel furnace at the Ashland facility capable of producing a higher grade of iron.[27]

The Worthington Cylinders division, meanwhile, offered two lines of low-pressure cylinders and worked with Buckeye to introduce two new products: the Worthington Carry-Out Beer Keg, a stainless steel container with a plastic footring and collar molded by the plastics operations,[28] and "Balloon Time," a disposable helium container packaged with party balloons and sold through major distributors like Kmart and Wal-Mart.[29]

The fourth division, cast steel, wasn't faring so well.[30] Traditionally, the castings market depended on the rollercoaster fortunes of the railroad industry. "In a good year that's about 95 percent of our business," Malenick said.

"In a down year, it's probably 88 to 90 percent of our sales. So a big part of our sales at Buckeye rides the cycles of the railroad industry, and

This page: Hurt by a slump in demand for railcars, Buckeye moved into new businesses, winning contracts for defense and mass transit. Buckeye's business fortunes, however, depended on the railcar industry. Buckeye produced many parts for railcars, including couplers (inset). Below, a worker is chipping roughness from a subway undercarriage.

you'll have two or three good years where you're really going well, and then you'll have two or three years where you're really down. The markets just collapse. Those lean years are really lean, and the good years are really good."[31]

Shortly after Worthington acquired Buckeye International in 1980, however, the railroad industry fell into a prolonged slump. As John H. McConnell recalls, Buckeye Steel Castings produced components for many of the 96,000 railcars (a record never repeated) produced in 1980. The next year, only 20,000 railcars were produced.[32] By 1984, companies began dropping out of the castings business in droves, and Worthington captured new business by cutting costs and aggressively seeking new markets. That year, Buckeye was the only U.S. company licensed to produce the leading design of undercarriages used in subway cars and commuter trains.

The coated glass venture, operated through ACT and run by Jack Deyo, was also proving to be a disappointment. Coated glass had been such a success in the 1970s that too many companies

entered the market. Supply soon surpassed demand, and prices plummeted. Furthermore, ACT lost ground to competitors working with a newer, higher speed coating technology.[33] ACT products had been used on more than 400 commercial buildings throughout the country, but Worthington began looking to sell the subsidiary.

"We had some problems and tried to turn it around," said Harold "Butch" Dell, who replaced

Deyo as general manager of the plant. "But it was obvious the business couldn't continue long-term."[34]

Worthington sold ACT in 1987, leading McConnell to remark that, in retrospect, entering the reflective glass market was a "mistake."[35] This decision to sell a non-core business and concentrate on core competencies would prove a valuable lesson in Worthington's future.

National Rolling Mills

Worthington, a steel processor first and foremost, was always looking to expand its core operations. Early in 1984, Worthington found a good opportunity and soon announced another acquisition. This time, the company sought to purchase National Rolling Mills, a leading custom processor of flat rolled steel and manufacturer of its own line of high quality suspension ceiling systems.[36]

It was a good value, Worthington believed, both for its location in the Northeast and for the opportunity to enter the high-growth suspended ceiling market.

Located in Malvern, Pennsylvania, a suburb of Philadelphia, NRM had a history similar to Worthington's own. In 1946, NRM's John H. "Jack" McCoy had set up shop as an aluminum warehousing operation in a converted garage with a modest $3,000 investment.[37] In 1951, McCoy and 10 other investors incorporated and expanded the business

Above: In 1984, Worthington bought National Rolling Mills as a way to enter the suspended ceiling grid business. National Rolling Mills produced the framework used to support the acoustical ceiling tiles common to large buildings.

Below left: In the 1980s, Worthington also began producing steel ingots at Buckeye. These special-alloy, high-quality ingots were sold to steel producers.

by roll-forming steel. Manufacturing of acoustical suspension ceiling grid began a year later.

After the acquisition, Worthington gained 400,000 square feet of plant space on 40 acres near Philadelphia and six distribution centers in Florida, Georgia, Illinois, North Carolina, Ohio and Texas.[38] The steel mill division pickled, slit and cold-reduced hot-rolled steel into coils of various gauges and widths. NRM could also zinc-coat steel for rust-resistant applications. The mill electro-galvanized steel by passing each coil through cells where a specially controlled chemical coating of zinc was applied to both sides. The coil coating line painted two sides simultaneously in a wide range of finishes.

This coating was used in the production of acoustical suspension ceiling grid, which was National Rolling Mills' largest product line. The acoustical division produced a complete line of suspended ceiling systems and accessories for all types and sizes of concealed and lay-in pane ceiling. These products were supplied in a wide range of colors and finishes and could be found in both residential and commercial buildings. Finished products were marketed through authorized acoustical distributors and contractors and to manufacturers of ceiling tile. More than 31,000 tons of light-gauge painted and electro-painted steel were converted to ceiling grids each year.

Ralph Roberts, who was then serving as general manager of Worthington Steel–Chicago, was transferred to the Malvern facility shortly after the acquisition. It was his fourth move in eight years. Under the arrangement, John McCoy would serve out his contract and Roberts would act as vice president and general manager. Roberts later remembered the kind of welcome he received:

"They didn't want anyone from Worthington coming in and running it. The first day I got there, the guard made me sign in. I went in and met the president at that time, Jack McCoy, who was the owner of the company, and Jack said to me, 'No

young man 38 years old is going to come in here and run this steel mill.' I said, 'Jack, you've got to understand. Don Malenick and Ed Ferkany have the faith in me. We're going to run this, and we're going to start transitioning the people to our Worthington philosophy.' Because those are our secret formulas, if there are any."[39]

After McCoy's retirement, Roberts was named executive vice president for both steel and acoustical ceilings. Bringing Malvern into the Worthington fold was a complex task. The mill was unionized, and unlike the plants at Baltimore and Chicago, the workers did not vote to decertify. Also, the sheer size of the operation — 600 employees on a 38-acre site — resisted a quick transition to the Worthington way.

National Rolling Mills' plant in Malvern, Pennsylvania. This plant featured the nation's most advanced electrolytic nickel line, which was used to produce a wide variety of finishes, including the corrosion-resistant steel used to coat batteries.

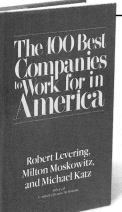

"We knew we had to start getting the philosophy in place," said Roberts. "We thought and felt they had good skill sets as far as manufacturing, but it was just the way we wanted to treat the people."[40]

Getting Noticed

It was a rough decade for steel in the 1980s, but Worthington was able to post the numbers it did because of hard work, flexibility in its employees and manufacturing, and its adherence to tight financial principles. "We were very lean," remembered Bruce Ruhl, who was in investor relations throughout much of the 1980s.

"And 8 a.m. was our starting point. I remember once we were out late celebrating an associate's birthday and I moseyed on in here I think at a few minutes to eight. And Mr. McConnell was right in here with his hand over the threshold. You know, just wanted to make sure we started at eight. No matter how late we were up, we had to be ready to hit the deck and the reason for that is clear. We expect people to be here and be accessible."[41]

It was a hard-working company, but Worthington employees — who were directly responsible for the company's success — were considered among the luckiest in America. In February 1984, Worthington was named one of *The 100 Best Companies to Work for in America* by authors Robert Levering, Milton

Moskowitz and Michael Katz, who selected companies on the basis of pay, benefits, job security and camaraderie.[42]

In its 1985 review of metals, *Forbes* magazine also singled out Worthington, the only one of 36 companies to have a positive five-year growth rate in earnings per share, as having a "brighter future" than any other company in the industry.[43]

Worthington also continued to advance its position on the *Fortune* 500. Based on 1985 sales, it ranked 385th with sales of $700.7 million. Moreover, between 1975 and 1985, the compa-

Above: Worthington Industries structured its employee relations on respect, flexibility, integrity and profit sharing. As a result, Worthington was the most productive company in the steel industry and was featured as one of the best companies in the United States to work for in this 1984 book.

Right: In 1985, John H. McConnell built an athletic facility at the Columbus Worthington Industries Industrial Park. Open to all employees and their families, the center was an extension of the Worthington Wellness Program and featured events coordinated by the local YMCA.

Worthington Steel–Jackson, based in Jackson, Michigan, joined Worthington in 1985 when the company bought Jackson Steel Service.

ny's 32.8 percent return placed it in the top six percent of all *Fortune* 1,000 companies.[44]

This kind of prosperity allowed John P. McConnell, who had moved into the personnel department, to realize a personal ambition. He approached his father with the idea of building an athletic center. The idea was approved and the facility was soon constructed at the Worthington Industrial Park complex in Columbus. It was open to all Worthington employees and their families, with activities coordinated by members of the YMCA.[45] The center served as a complement to the Worthington Wellness Program as "an action plan to preserve our most important asset — people."[46]

The Wellness Program was designed to lessen the risk of serious and long-term illnesses by encouraging positive lifestyle changes, something the athletically minded McConnell had always believed in. Through the program, Worthington employees had access to free educational materials on topics such as smoking cessation, weight

loss, prevention and diagnosis of heart disease, cancer, and exercise. The company also regularly brought in health care professionals to provide routine testing for such conditions as high blood pressure and diabetes.

Investing in Its Business:
Jackson and Newman-Crosby

Worthington's dollar investment in its people was matched only by its investment in future growth. Between 1984 and 1986, the company funneled about $68.7 million into capital expenditures.[47] Annealing capacity at Columbus was increased by nearly half.[48] An expansion at the Monroe pickling facility shortened lead time, which pleased customers who had adopted new inventory control programs like Just-In-Time.[49]

The company also continued to look for good acquisitions and, in April 1985, bought Jackson Steel Service, Inc., located in central Michigan. The 100-employee company had established a solid customer base and a good reputation throughout the upper Midwest.[50]

When it was bought by Worthington, John Cummings, who had been working outside sales for a large region in Michigan, moved to the new Jackson facility as vice president of sales and later became operations manager. "Like the other plants, this plant was geographically matched to a region," Cummings said. "If we had a sale out of here that we couldn't produce, it was something that Columbus could do, and they would charge us a price for the steel and all the processing cost, plus profit."[51]

Soon after, Worthington announced another acquisition, this time of the privately owned Newman-Crosby Steel, Inc.[52] Newman had both a rich past and a troubled present. It had begun operating in New York City in 1910 under the name D.J. Crosby Company but relocated to Pawtucket, Rhode Island, in 1914. The company produced cold rolled strip steel, flat wire, and special shapes in low carbon, carbon spring steel and alloy grades for industry. Of its 150 people, 125 were hourly production workers represented by the United Steelworkers of America, AFL-CIO.[53]

Newman-Crosby products were sold primarily to the transmission chain, business machine, fastener, automotive, jewelry, clothing spring maker, appliance and job stamper industries.[54] Sales were concentrated in New England, the Midwest, the Middle Atlantic and the South, with occasional shipments to the West Coast, Mexico and Taiwan. About 65 percent of the company's business was in flat rolled strip, with the remainder in special shapes and edges.

The company had several rolling mills capable of reducing hot rolled bands from .187 inch down to .006 inch. It also had two flat-wire mills and a wire-draw block used for converting rod into wire and wire into flats and rolling specialized shapes to close tolerance. A variety of slitters were used for converting material widths to very close tolerance.[55]

Although Newman had not turned a profit for a long time, it broadened Worthington's product line by giving access to the light gauge, high carbon and alloy strip markets, as well as moving the company into New England.[56] Also, Newman could produce very narrow material with different types of edges.

Opening in Midland

In fall 1985, Worthington broke ground for a new 80,000-square-foot manufacturing facility in Midland, Georgia.[57] Lying on a 48-acre plot just east of Columbus, Georgia, the facility was designed to house both the Worthington cylinder division and a steel coil slitting operation to be run under the guidance of Worthington Steel–Rock Hill.[58] The Georgia location was chosen to better accommodate one of Cylinders' best customers, the W.C. Bradley

Like the plant in Claremore, Oklahoma, Worthington's plant in Midland, Georgia, was equipped with both processing and cylinder manufacturing capabilities. Midland was managed from Worthington Steel–Rock Hill.

Company of Columbus, Georgia, makers of Char-Broil gas grills.

In November, 20 employees of the cylinder division were relocated from the Ohio and Oklahoma facilities to help open the Midland operation. Management and hourly employees worked around plumbers, electricians, welders and laborers who hadn't quite finished construction. Major equipment included a 600-ton press purchased from Peugeot of France and die tooling, welding and pressure testing equipment designed by Worthington's own engineering department and manufactured at Capital Die Tool in Columbus, Ohio. A state-of-the-art polyurethane paint system was installed to coat the cylinders with the most durable finish available in the marketplace.

Under the direction of the Rock Hill managers, the slitter operation at Midland occupied about one-third of the new building. A railroad spur entered the building to the rear to help accommodate large steel shipments. Because of a slumping Western market, the slitter previously located

in Claremore came to Midland along with several key personnel.[59]

The Georgia location soon proved its worth; After only a few months in operation, the Midland facility began winning contracts that hadn't been viable previously because of high freight costs.

Specialty Processing

Soon after Midland opened, Worthington forged a new concept in the steel processing industry when it announced a joint venture with U.S. Steel to build and operate a toll-processing facility in Jackson, Michigan.[60] To be run by Worthington with production dedicated for U.S. Steel, the plant would process wide sheet-steel for markets previously served by the major mills.

A greenfield operation, Midland featured a sophisticated slitting operation that occupied almost one-third of the plant.

Shown under construction, Worthington Specialty Processing was a unique joint venture between U.S. Steel and Worthington. In the Michigan facility, Worthington toll-processed steel for the giant steel company.

The venture was part of a survival strategy for Big Steel: to outsource finishing work to companies able to do a better job.[61]

Paul Hocter, a production supervisor and one of 25 employees who transferred from Columbus to Jackson, remembered how the toll-processing arrangement was set up. "The way it was designed is that U.S. Steel would bring the sales and customer base, and we're responsible for managing it," he said. "We didn't own the material, so essentially, we were selling them time."[62]

Worthington Specialty Processing began operating in August 1986 with a 600,000-ton capacity.[63] Located on a 40-acre plot south of Jackson, the three-bay, 150,000-square-foot plant housed two state-of-the-art 72-inch slitting lines and one sophisticated 72-inch cut-to-length line for blanking capabilities.[64] All the equipment was designed to process the extremely critical zinc-coated exterior body panels used by automakers.[65]

"We are excited about expanding our steel-processing expertise into the markets served by the major mills," said John H. McConnell. "We believe that processing of high quality sheet steel in large volume will be an area of rapid growth in the years ahead."[66]

The partnership between Worthington — the superstar of processors — and integrated king U.S. Steel seemed representative of the changes in the steel industry throughout the 1980s. Faced with formidable competition from overseas, as well as from processors, service centers and minimills in the U.S., Big Steel had no choice but to reinvent itself. Their dominance of the industry a thing of the past, integrated mills sought niches of their own.

By the latter years of the decade, the U.S. steel industry was symbolized by that depressing sight, the abandoned mill. Indeed, in Rust Belt cities like Youngstown, Ohio, and Buffalo, New York, idle plants and laid-off steel workers

MCCONNELL'S FOUNTAIN

O N JULY 4, 1986, THE CITY OF Columbus, Ohio, dedicated a new floating fountain in the Scioto River to John H. McConnell.[1] The $50,000 lighted fountain, which shot a spray of water 100 feet into the air, was donated by 6,000 employees of Worthington Industries, many of whom attended the ceremony at the downtown Riverfront amphitheater. Columbus Mayor Dana G. "Buck" Rhinehart paid tribute to McConnell, calling him a "man that stands out as a diamond" in the city.

"We realized that John McConnell had done an awful lot for our city," said Rhinehart, "and we had never really stopped to say, 'Thank you.'"[2]

On July 4, 1986, more than 6,000 employees of Worthington Industries presented the John H. McConnell fountain to the people of Columbus. McConnell, right, sits with former Ohio Governer James A. Rhodes. In addition, hundreds of Columbus citizens (inset) watched the ceremony.

were an everyday phenomenon. Yet, as Christopher Hall writes, the image represented only the troubles of the integrated mills. It "ignored new realities of successful steel business thriving in previously unlikely places. Specialty steel companies, making stainless and complex alloy steels; new minimills in the South and upper Midwest; and downstream steel processors and service centers, undertaking value-added and distribution functions the mills could no longer afford to do, made money and expanded."[67]

Worthington was one of the new-breed steel companies, and John H. McConnell thanked Worthington employees for making the company a success: "Your strong competitive spirit and ability to meet the demands imposed on us by customers, suppliers and competitors have played a major role in establishing us as the leader in our industry."

However, McConnell warned, Worthington could not afford to be complacent:

"[W]ith competition now coming from all parts of the globe and customers accepting nothing less than the best in quality and pricing, the challenges of today's markets are far more difficult than those of the past. If our recognition as one of the premier companies in the country is to continue, we must make sure our quality and service stand for excellence worldwide....

"With the loss of thousands of jobs in recent months due to the financial failures of major U.S. corporations, including those in the steel industry, it is obvious only the most prepared of companies will grow and prosper.... If we fail to recognize the seriousness of the challenges at hand, we could find ourselves drowning without realizing we are in the water."[68]

Throughout the 1980s, as the steel industry was crippled by foreign competition, Worthington counted on profit from its cylinder operation.

CHAPTER SEVEN

RIDING THE RECOVERY

1987–1989

"We regularly hear so-called 'experts' say that the entrepreneurial spirit is dead, that American workers have lost their will to work and that our industry cannot compete with foreign manufacturers. Some are even questioning the merits of the very system upon which our nation was built. The people of Worthington Industries do not share these doubts."

— John H. McConnell, 1988[1]

IN 1987, WORTHINGTON INDUSTRIES set sales and earnings records for the 26th consecutive year, with almost $819 million in sales and $42.1 million in earnings. Yet company leaders were still unsatisfied.[2]

"While these results were good in light of certain market situations," John H. McConnell wrote, "the rate of growth was less than we expect over the long term."[3] Both McConnell and President Don Malenick admitted to having "mixed feelings" about the year's results: "While not disappointed with record earnings, we can do better and intend to do so."[4]

The "market situations" to which McConnell referred included a worldwide slump in demand, a sudden upswing in the domestic market and concessions granted to the integrated mills that "muddled" pricing for steel processors.[5] By the mid-1980s, the global market for raw steel was dangerously soft. Production capacity outstripped demand by more than 100 million tons, a figure nearly equal to the annual rate of U.S. consumption.[6]

This situation was complicated by foreign steel, which had begun pouring into the country in the early 1980s. In 1984, to protect themselves, the debilitated integrated mills won increased trade protection in the form of Voluntary Restraint Agreements, which limited the amount of steel imported from foreign manufacturers.[7] The Reagan administration, however, required that the inte-

grated mills meet certain provisions. Trade restraints, according to author Ahlbrandt, in *The Renaissance of American Steel*, "were put in place for a five-year period, but they were subject to annual review.

"Extensions would be granted year by year, and then only if the industry invested most of its net cash flow from steel operations in capital improvements and allocated about 1 percent of net cash flow for worker retraining. In return for reducing imports, the industry was required to modernize, and it did. Billions were invested in technologies that helped make the industry more efficient and improve the quality of American steel."[8]

Trade restrictions bought time for the integrated mills, but they translated to higher material costs for steel users and processors like Worthington. To complicate the situation, a six-month strike at USX weakened the supply of steel in the United States at the same time that foreign steel was kept out of the country, and an unex-

Worthington Custom Products expanded to meet competition, opening up a plant in Cumming, Georgia, in 1989. From there, the company made products like the control panel for this washing machine.

Although a disappointment in terms of growth, 1987 was another record year — partly thanks to healthy sales of cylinders used for backyard barbecues. This major market for Worthington Cylinders had begun to develop in the 1970s.

pected surge in domestic demand further tightened the market. Combined, these forces drove up prices for Worthington.

When USX returned to full-scale production, Worthington expected the price of raw steel would again decline. This prevented Worthington (and other processing companies) from raising its prices because it had to stay competitive after the strike ended. So despite improved market share and increased sales, Worthington was unable to recoup its material losses.[9] Processed steel sales rose 8 percent to $32 million, but pretax earnings declined $4.2 million, or 8 percent.[10]

The slowdown affected other business segments as well. As Detroit automakers dealt with rising material costs, Worthington Custom Products grew a meager 1 percent, and net earnings dropped 7 percent.[11] Similarly, despite a moderate increase in sales of pipe fittings, stiff competition drove prices down, and a second factory shift cost Worthington training and start-up fees.[12] These factors depleted earnings for the pipe fittings segment, which fell $600,000 on the heels of a $1.7 million dip the previous year.[13]

Offsetting these difficulties, however, were solid gains in both steel castings and cylinders. Strong growth in mass transit shipments and steel ingot production and a modest upturn in the freight railcar market generated a 40 percent jump in earnings for steel castings.[14] In pressure cylinders, sales rose 8 percent to $4.6 million, and earnings were up 23 percent to $9.5 million.[15] Because of an especially hot summer, refrigerant cylinders sold briskly, and sales in world markets picked up as the value of the U.S. dollar declined.

Although 1987 wasn't a bad year, it was unspectacular — frustrating for a company accustomed to spectacular growth. As Robert Borel commented, "We've never had the major crises, business crises, that a lot of companies have in terms of major layoffs [or] in terms of major downsizings.... A 'crisis' for us is when we don't earn more money this year than we did the last year."[16]

John H. McConnell: Outstanding Alum

There were, however, plenty of non-financial good tidings in 1987. John H. McConnell was chosen by Michigan State University as one of the year's "Outstanding Alums," the highest honor bestowed on graduates who had distinguished themselves in their careers, professional associations and communities.[17] Selected by the Business Alumni Association Awards Committee, McConnell was honored alongside Richard Cregar, president of three Detroit area food service operations, and Robert Stempel, executive vice president of General Motors.

Only a couple months later, "Mr. Mac" became "Dr. Mac" when he was granted an honorary doctorate of humanities by Ashland College, a private university with a distinguished business school and the same hometown as Worthington's pipe fittings division.[18] The honor was presented during commencement ceremonies, where McConnell told the

1988 graduating class, "Today is a very special occasion. Since I did not attend my own graduation [at Michigan State] because I had a job and went back to West Virginia, this is the first time I've ever had on a cap and gown."[19]

By spring 1988, Worthington Industries itself had reason to celebrate. Market conditions were finally improving, and the company enjoyed four straight quarters of record sales and earnings.[20] Sales topped $904.2 million, and earnings rose 33 percent over the previous year.[21]

This strength was reflected across all of Worthington's divisions. In processed steel, where USX had finally resumed operations, sales rose 16 percent.[22] Demand had also picked up across a variety of industries, including automotive, appliance and computer. In addition, Worthington was helped by the joint venture with U.S. Steel at Jackson, Michigan, which proved "solidly profitable" in its first full year of operation.[23]

Metal Flo Acquisition Moves Worthington Manufacturing Abroad

Company officers continued looking for ways to expand, and on May 17, 1988, Worthington Cylinders announced the acquisition of Metal Flo Corporation of Guelph, Ontario. Renamed Worthington Cylinders of

In Jackson, Michigan, Worthington Specialty Processing, a joint venture with U.S. Steel, celebrated its first full year of operation in 1988. That year, the new company turned a profit.

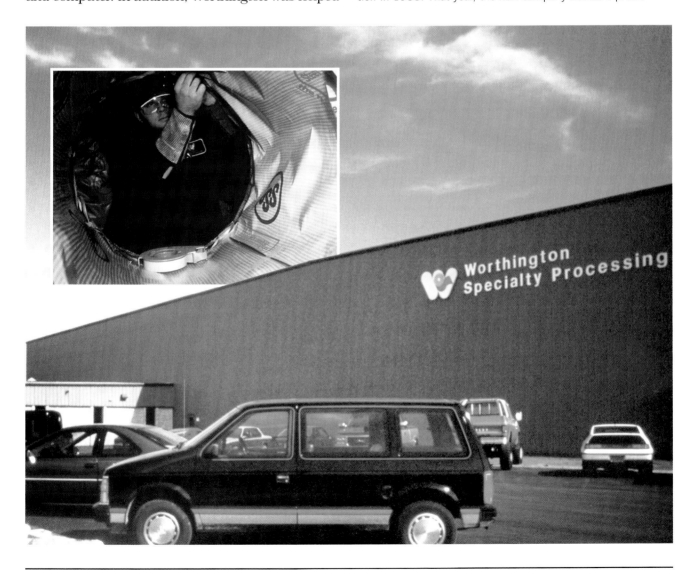

Above and below: In 1988, Worthington bought Metal Flo Corporation, based in Ontario. This acquisition added a major cylinder manufacturer to the company's portfolio and was Worthington's first attempt to manufacture cylinders outside the United States.

Canada, the 45,000-square-foot plant manufactured a variety of large-capacity propane and acetylene cylinders for portable heating and cooking, welding, and brazing. Shortly after the acquisition, Worthington expanded the operation into the recreation and recreational vehicles markets.[24]

Worthington Cylinders of Canada expanded Worthington's manufacturing capabilities to include larger cylinders, opened new markets for existing products and was the first attempt to manufacture outside U.S. borders. In early July, 45 members of the Canadian facility visited Columbus for a "Welcome Aboard" celebration and an introduction to the Worthington way.[25]

Later that summer, on July 14, 1988, Worthington debuted on Standard & Poor's 500 Stock Index. The company's stock immediately increased by $1.125 per share to $24.375 per share amid a wave of trading, making it the second most active stock on the NASDAQ.[26]

"It's a milestone to achieve that recognition," Worthington vice president Joseph Stegmayer told *The Columbus Dispatch.* "We are very pleased to be on it, and we think it will give us some more expo-

London Industries, founded in London, Ohio, in 1988, was a joint venture with two Japanese companies. The company produced a variety of plastic components, primarily for the domestic and foreign auto industries.

sure to the investment community as a whole. Some money management companies only buy stocks that are on the S&P 500, so once you get on there, you become more visible."[27]

The Recovery at Home

Also that summer, Worthington formed a partnership with two Japanese companies to build an injection-molded plastics manufacturing plant called London Industries in London, Ohio.[28] Worthington held a 60 percent interest, and the rest was divided between Nissen Chemical Industry, a supplier of plastic parts and components to the automobile industry, and Sumitomo Corporation of America, a trading company. The company purchased a vacant 155,600-square-foot plant.[29]

Having Japanese as partners, McConnell believed, would help Worthington develop closer business relationships with Japanese subsidiaries in the United States. By the late 1980s, Japanese manufacturing companies were establishing a presence in the United States at a rapid pace — too rapid, according to some Americans. Yet these Japanese companies were lean and efficient, posing a serious competitive threat to aging Big Steel

behemoths, which were helplessly watching their market share and revenue dwindle.

This trend, which didn't show any signs of abating, had two effects: An intensive "Buy American" campaign was launched nationwide by the media and politicians; and, perhaps more importantly, American companies began studying their successful Japanese counterparts.

They proved apt students. By the end of the 1980s, the domestic steel industry had plowed billions back into its businesses and restructured.[30] It appeared that a turnaround was imminent, something that would have seemed impossible only a few years before.

"Steel, America's wounded industrial giant through much of this decade, has been on a surprising two-year comeback," wrote *The Detroit Free Press* in September 1988. "The companies are making money, the surviving mills are hustling at 90 percent capacity, the imports' share of the market is declining, and there is a spirit of optimism in the industry."[31]

Signs of recovery were everywhere. National Steel posted a $47.8 million profit in 1987 after suffering a $59.8 million loss in 1986.[32] A year later, Rouge Steel, then a subsidiary of Ford Motor Company, posted its first profitable year

Inside the London Industries plant, employees worked with customers to develop products, then used injection molding presses (top) to shape plastic resin into hundreds of products. The finished items were treated with a range of finishes (below).

in a decade. USX recorded a $370 million profit for the first half of 1988,[33] more than it had earned in any full year since 1981.[34]

To explain the resurgence of American steel, analysts pointed to several factors: improved productivity, the practice of outsourcing value-added processes to specialists like Worthington, continued import controls, the falling value of the dollar, and simple luck because domestic demand had swelled while capacity was shrinking.

Thomas Graham, president of U.S. Steel, insisted that the major credit be given to the mills themselves, which had emerged leaner and meaner.

"There are multiple factors behind our improved financial results. But neither [the import quotas] nor the devalued dollar has been the primary factor. The changed conditions which the domestic steel industry is enjoying are principally the changed conditions which the domestic steel industry has implemented."[35]

In *The Renaissance of American Steel*, authors Ahlbrandt, Fruehan and Giarratani concurred:

"The traditional firms that still dominate the popular image of steelmaking have shed unprofitable operations, reorganized production to eliminate waste and focused their resources in terms both of product lines and of the geographic markets they serve. Industry change has been caused by international as well as domestic competitive pressure."[36]

Between 1975 and 1995, twenty-seven of the original 48 integrated mills in the United States were closed or operated as nonintegrated plants. Meanwhile, the remaining ones boasted impressive efficiency.[37] In 1988, American steelmakers required less than six worker hours to produce a ton of steel, in contrast to the 10.1 hours required in 1982.[38] The integrated mills were now "comparable with [mills] anywhere in the world, and better than Japan and Europe," according to American Iron & Steel Institute (AISI) President Milton Deaner.[39]

To survive, Big Steel had won concessions from union workers.

"There were wage and benefit givebacks by union and hourly workers that amounted to $2 billion in 1983 alone, and this was followed by more givebacks in 1986. Work rules were loosened and job classifications made less restrictive to give the companies greater flexibility on the plant floor, thereby increasing efficiency. Big Steel sought joint ventures and alliances with foreign steel producers. Capital investments were made to increase the efficiency of existing facilities. Firms diversified to other industries in attempts to improve financial performance, and they reorganized and focused steel operations."[40]

In effect, the big mills became "niche" producers, much like Worthington had already been able to do. U.S. Steel, for example, abandoned unprofitable avenues such as rod production in favor of flat-rolling steel for the auto and appliance industries. By 1991, the company that had suffered a $600 million operating loss in 1983 — about $75 on each ton shipped — was the top performer in the integrated sector.[41]

Why Worthington's Way Worked

Some of the changes implemented by the integrated mills vindicated the innovations upon which McConnell had founded his company more than three decades earlier. In 1988, Worthington officers presented an overview of how the company had escaped the troubles of the integrated mills:

"Many companies that experienced boom times during the 1950s and 1960s, an era of high demand and sparse competition, became fat and happy. In some corporations there evolved a bureaucratic system that rivaled that of the United States government. Nothing was attempted without first running it through layer upon layer of corporate management, which greatly inhibited substantive action....

"Fortunately, American business has begun to address these problems within the framework of free enterprise. As the economy slowed in the early 1980s, firms began to put their houses in order. They realized they could not continue business as usual with bloated payrolls and unproductive procedures. Many have taken steps to reduce fixed costs, improve work rules and increase productivity. Throughout America, companies have met foreign competition head-on and are becoming stronger than ever.

"Many of the positive programs now being implemented by other American businesses have always been fundamental to the Worthington way. We 'keep it simple.' We have never had such roadblocks to progress as organization charts, chains of command and strict lines of communication. Noted author Tom Peters recently asked, 'How do you manage a six-thousand-person organization with literally no formal policies or procedures to follow?' Mr. McConnell replied, 'We have developed a unique management principle — we talk to each other.'"[42]

The Shield Drops

This recovery had, at least in part, been helped by the import controls that had been imposed on foreign steel. By protecting the domestic market, the U.S. government had given steel producers the breathing room necessary to retool. By 1989, however, the five-year VRAs were about to expire. Naturally, domestic producers didn't want to lose their protection and sought ways to maintain trade barriers. The AISI, representing about 80 percent of the industry, advocated another five-year extension, arguing that the extra time was needed for foreign countries to reduce excess capacity and avoid the temptation to "dump" steel in the United States.[43]

The issue became a hot button of the 1988 general election. On one side were U.S. Steel, Bethlehem and the United Steelworkers union; on the other, steel-using companies like Caterpillar and mills partly owned by Japanese interests. In summer 1988, *Fortune* magazine surveyed 218 of the country's top CEOs on the question of international competition and protectionism. By a three-to-one margin, the CEOs rejected the "trendy doomsayers of decline" and insisted that American industry had learned its lesson and was gaining on foreign competitors. "Their overwhelming preference," wrote *Fortune*, "is for open borders, not protectionism."[44]

Among the 81 percent of CEOs who agreed that protectionism "stifles innovation and creativity" was John H. McConnell. The Worthington chief believed that U.S. officials should learn from the Japanese government's overactive role in helping industry.[45] The domestic regulatory burden was hampering American industrial might, McConnell told *Fortune*, which noted that "[t]he Columbus steel processor now spends over $500,000 each year to comply with recently imposed government regulations."[46]

McConnell had a chance to air his views when then–presidential candidate George Bush made Buckeye Steel Castings a campaign stop on September 16, 1988.[47] The man who would soon be president spent several hours touring Buckeye, addressing employees and meeting with company managers and local political leaders. The visit was something of a return to his roots for Bush, whose grandfather had joined Buckeye in 1901 and served as president for nearly 20 years.[48]

In the end, the new Bush administration forged a compromise between the free-trade and protectionist camps. Rather than granting the full five-year VRA extension sought by the integrated mills, the government extended trade restrictions for 30 months and launched an initiative to negotiate an international steel consensus agreement to remove trade-distorting practices. By the time the VRAs expired in 1992, American steelmakers had established a firmer foundation from which to compete with international mills. The steel industry shake-up, while at times troubling and even tragic, had the end result of improving the state of steelmaking worldwide.[49]

As Don Malenick pointed out, "The quality of steel today is, without a doubt, the best quality that's ever been produced anytime in the history of mankind.... At one time when they talked about world-class, people thought it was strictly price. But there's price. There's quality. And there's service."[50]

Breaking the Billion Dollar Barrier

In September 1988, midway through the fiscal year, John H. McConnell had a piece of good news for shareholders, who were used to hearing good news from Worthington. The company was expected to soon enter the ranks of the nation's billion-dollar companies in terms of annual revenue.[51]

"We have the equipment in place, the facilities in place, and the people in place to be a $1 billion

As it neared the $1 billion mark, Worthington counted among its largest customers the Big Three automotive companies. Worthington produced everything from dashboard components to auto body parts to seat belt connectors (pictured).

company this year," he said at the annual share-holders meeting. "That's been our goal for some time. Unless there is a downturn in the economy … we will get to one billion."[52]

In making this prediction, McConnell was on firm ground. During the quarter ending August 31, 1988, Worthington recorded net revenues of $226.5 million, 14 percent ahead of the same period a year earlier.[53]

Toll Processing in Taylor

In 1989, still enjoying healthy profits from its toll-processing joint venture with USX, Worthington built another toll-processing facility in Taylor, Michigan.[54] Toll processing was an attractive, albeit risky, growth area for Worthington. Although it made money, it naturally followed the same market cycles the rest of the steel industry does.[55]

"The good news for us is that we carry no inventory, so we have no inventory costs," explained Ed Ferkany. "The bad news is that you're not necessarily selling big numbers. The sales figures are not as great as they would be if we were buying product and reselling it, but the process charges we send back to the mills are adequate if we have a high volume."[56]

In April 1989, Worthington acquired a 65,000-square-foot plastic injection molding plant in Cumming, Georgia.[57] The former home of Fame Plastics, the Georgia plant produced components for appliance, automotive and lawn equipment customers in the Southeast market.[58]

An Almost Acquisition

A few weeks later, Worthington made headlines when another potential acquisition was leaked to the Detroit media. On May 3, *The Detroit Free Press* reported that Worthington and Ford Motor Company were in "advanced" negotiations for the sale of Rouge Steel, a cornerstone of the Rouge complex in Dearborn, Michigan, and the eighth largest integrated steel mill in the country.[59]

The deal would have profoundly changed Worthington Industries. In Rouge Steel, Worthington saw a chance to guarantee its processing facilities a steady supply of hot rolled steel even in times of tight supply. Furthermore, the company would enter new markets — notably outer bodies for automobiles — that depended on the capability of hot rolling metal from slabs into coils. Rouge's location in the same sprawling complex as Ford's Mustang assembly plant, engine plant and metal stamping factory provided an automatically intimate relationship with the auto industry.

Although neither Worthington nor Ford would make a public statement, Harry Lester, director of United Steelworkers District 29, told *The Detroit Free Press* that a joint venture comprised of Worthington and a foreign steelmaker was trying to purchase Rouge Steel. Talk of the sale met immediate opposition from Rouge's union workforce. UAW Local 600 President Bob King called the prospect of a sale to Worthington "particularly upsetting" because of what he called the company's "antiunion history."[60] Lester complained of the "heavy opposition" the Steelworkers had faced when trying to organize Worthington's Taylor and Jackson plants.[61] However, John Green, a Steelworkers union subdirector in Columbus, told the reporter the company had had "no problem" coexisting with unions in its five organized facilities.[62] The *Free Press* also mentioned a 1985 article in *Mother Jones* magazine that had lauded Worthington as one of the best companies to work for in America because of its "commitment to fairness, product and environmental quality, ethics, and people."[63]

In Taylor, Michigan, Worthington converted a warehouse into a state-of-the-art steel processing plant. Similar to the plant in Jackson, this facility was used as a toll-processing facility for integrated steel producers.

Coincidentally, Worthington was in the middle of a struggle with union officials at its Newman-Crosby Steel plant. Before joining Worthington Industries, Newman-Crosby had been unprofitable for some time. However, as Malenick wrote in the company newsletter, Worthington had felt that "with the help and cooperation of the workforce," its years of marketing and operating experience in the steel industry would soon make Newman profitable.[64] Also, Worthington had invested in upgrading the plant's equipment. Malenick wrote:

"As Newman continued to struggle and lose money, it was obvious changes were necessary. For that reason, we approached the leadership of the unionized workforce. Our goal was to see

In April 1989, Worthington Custom Products opened this plant in Cumming, Georgia. Previously the site of Fame Plastics, the plant produced parts for appliances, cars, and lawn and garden equipment.

what we could do together to keep the company alive and, most importantly, preserve the jobs of its people. Many conversations took place over a period of several months. In the end, the leadership refused to work with us to make the necessary changes."[65]

On June 28, 1989, after three unprofitable years for Newman-Crosby, Worthington shut down the Newman facility.[66] It was a devastating failure for a company not used to failing. "Our experience with Newman was not pleasant," wrote Malenick, but "the history of Newman as a member of the Worthington team gives us a valuable learning experience to draw on in the future."[67]

The future was now. Facing an uproar of opposition from both the UAW and the Steelworkers, Worthington dropped its bid for the Rouge Steel plant.[68] "The whole idea was a good one," McConnell told *The Columbus Dispatch* a few months later:

"We use a lot of hot rolled steel, and the market was such that we had a tough time getting it.... The

building [at Rouge] is modern, totally rebuilt. Everything is up to snuff. The one drawback for us was the labor situation. The UAW publicly stated that we were antiunion and that if we [tried to buy it] they would not allow it to happen. We just decided it would be foolish to go into a situation with a totally negative attitude from the workforce.[69]

Harold "Red" Poling, CEO of Ford Motor Company at the time, later talked about the almost deal and how close Worthington came to taking over part of Ford's steel operation. "The thing that caused that to be turned down was the union situation," Poling said. "I would have liked to see Worthington take that business because it would have done a great job."[70]

Ultimately, however, Worthington did not turn its back on Rouge entirely. The most attractive part of the aborted deal had been ensuring a consistent supply of hot rolled steel, so in December 1989, Worthington obtained a minority ownership position in Rouge by buying into Marico Acquisition Company, which was made up of four investors (including Ford) that purchased the 66-year-old steelworks.[71]

"We are not going to be involved with management. We are a shareholder," stated Worthington spokesman Mark Tikson.[72]

Under the agreement, Ford — which had threatened to turn the steelworks into a minimill and lay off half the workforce if a buyer couldn't be found — promised to purchase 800,000 tons a year from Rouge.[73] Worthington pledged to buy another 700,000 tons.[74]

In the midst of this maneuvering, Worthington Industries achieved the milestone that John H. McConnell had so recently predicted. On June 16, 1989, *The Columbus Dispatch* announced:

"Worthington Industries, Inc., has joined the ranks of Columbus' billion-dollar companies, chalking up record annual earnings to boot.

"The steel-processing company reported yesterday that it registered net sales and revenues of $1.01 billion for its fiscal year ended May 31....

"John H. McConnell, chairman and chief executive officer of the steel processing, plastics and cast products company, was thrilled. 'Fiscal 1989 was by far Worthington's best year ever.... Strong performances by all of our businesses helped us not only reach $1 billion in sales, but more importantly achieve our targeted 15 percent growth in earnings and 20 percent return on equity.'"[75]

In reaching the billion-dollar mark, Worthington joined the area's elite companies, including Wendy's International and The Limited, Inc. Productivity figures for 1989 were nothing less than extraordinary; Worthington registered $431,000 in sales per employee, compared with $135,000 in the metal manufacturing industry overall and $111,000 for all of U.S. manufacturing.[76]

Asked by a reporter why Worthington had become so successful, John H. McConnell contemplated the question as he examined the ever-present cigar he poised between two fingers. "We like to think we run it right," he answered.[77]

A "blank," or piece of steel preformed to exact specifications. Blanks were provided to the automotive industry through TWB Company, L.L.C., a Worthington joint venture based in Monroe, Michigan.

CHAPTER EIGHT

GOING GLOBAL

1990–1992

"There's a lot of entrepreneurialism in Worthington, even though it was founded in 1954.... Old industry can be as entrepreneurial as small organizations. Companies that don't think about what the future is going to present them might not be around in that future. Worthington ... today is trying to prepare itself to be a successful 21st century company."

— John Christie, president and COO, Worthington Industries[1]

I N 1990, THE NATION LAUNCHED its 10-year countdown to the millennium amid unsettling economic news. An economic slowdown was occurring, which President George Bush called a "temporary interruption in the longest peacetime expansion in American history."

"Things are pretty much back to normal," noted one business journal in January. "Unfortunately, that's bad news for steel producers."[2]

Reports showed rising wholesale prices and sluggish retail sales, and the Federal Reserve predicted slow growth in all sectors.[3] The stock market wobbled, then slid sharply, with the Dow Jones industrial average falling to a three-month low of 2,689.20 in the second week of January.[4]

In Ohio, the number of initial unemployment claims in December had jumped 41.3 percent statewide, the highest rate in five years. The majority of the new claims were made by laid-off workers in the auto industry, and another 65,000 lost their jobs in the first two weeks of January.[5]

This economic slump affected every industry served by steel, notably the automotive and appliance sectors. In 1991, the integrated mills lost an average of $44 per ton of steel shipped; one year later, the average loss "improved" to $26 per ton.[6] Worthington Industries, however, was coming off its best year ever. It had recently surpassed the billion-dollar sales milestone, and in 1990 enjoyed a "solid but unspectacular" year.[7]

"At Worthington Industries we expect to set earnings records every year," John H. McConnell and Don Malenick wrote to shareholders in 1990. "This year we did not achieve that goal."[8] In fact, sales slipped to $915.9 million, while earnings fell 12 percent to $55.2 million.

Worthington's best-performing business segments were steel castings, which was still flush with a 54 percent gain from the previous year, and suspension ceilings.[9] Railcar demand remained strong, and the recent acquisition of GSI Engineering, the leading United States–based design firm for railcar undercarriages, made the division a leader in technology and production capabilities. The suspension ceiling segment posted another record year in sales and earnings thanks to solid orders from the remodeling industry and new marketing in the Western states and Canada.[10]

The news was not as good for steel processing, which accounted for 71 percent of total sales

---

In 1990, Worthington celebrated its 35th anniversary. From a basement company with sales of $350,000, Worthington had grown into a $1 billion corporation.

and 80 percent of earnings. The general economy, which had been resilient in years past, slowed as consumers put a brake to strong demand. Nine months of low demand and wild pricing took its toll on sales and earnings. The pressure cylinder business also declined as cool spring weather and a carry-over of inventory reduced demand.[11]

Custom Products was also hit by the setback in the auto industry: Volume dropped as a result of slowing automobile production. Additionally, the startup costs of London Industries and the Georgia plant resulted in an earnings decline of 51 percent. Although Custom Products made up 18 percent of sales, it contributed only 9 percent of Worthington's earnings in 1990.[12]

The pipe fittings business, U-Brand, was also a casualty of the recession. Although the division was usually profitable, U-Brand had not produced returns consistent with Worthington's high goals. As a result, the facilities in Ashland and Puerto Rico were sold to the Mueller Brass Company in January of that year. Worthington's operating loss and loss on the sale of U-Brand totaled $2 million for the year.[13]

Celebrations in Order

Even with the depressed sales, Worthington Industries had plenty of reasons to celebrate in 1990. It was an anniversary year, and the company was in a solid financial position. Worthington had $50 million in cash and short-term investments and $180 million in working capital, and long-term debt was reduced to only 11 percent of total capital. Worthington had experienced 35 years of success in industries that "some characterize as mundane, even downright boring."[14]

Worthington had achieved an "enviable record" not because of a "major technological breakthrough or magic formula," said company officers, but through loyal adherence to its golden rule and "commitment to uncompromising quality and unsurpassed customer service. Growth has come from a variety of sources, including market share gains, development of new products and services, geographic expansions, and carefully selected acquisitions."[15]

Growth also had come from investment in itself. Between 1988 and 1990, the company had poured more than $100 million into capital improvement projects.[16]

To enhance the precision metals business, Worthington opened a 100,000-square-foot plant outside Nashville, Tennessee, in 1990. The plant featured highly advanced equipment for the manufacture of metal components to be used in power steering, transmission and antilock braking systems. The new company was called Worthington Precision Metals, Inc., and employed approximately 40 people.[17]

Going into Porter

Only a few months later, Worthington announced another major expansion: a state-

of-the-art processing and pickling facility in Porter, Indiana. This facility was designed to replace the venerable Worthington Steel–Chicago plant. According to Mark Stier, who went to Chicago as vice president of sales in 1984 and became general manager a year later, the company had planned to relocate the Chicago plant as early as the mid-1980s.

"It was a great little plant but landlocked," he remembered. "You just couldn't grow the business much more than it was."[18] In fact, it couldn't be grown at all. The plant was located so close to the runways at O'Hare International Airport that its windows shook when a plane approached.

"You'd be on the phone and you'd have to say 'Excuse me,' and wait," Stier said. "Ten seconds later you could get back on the phone."[19]

Worthington had begun searching for a new plant site as early as 1985 and finally found a 50-acre site in northwest Indiana, just east of Interstate 95.[20] Stier told *The Gary Post-Tribune* that the Porter location was chosen for its easy access to Detroit, Chicago and the Indiana mills.[21] "If you're going to be active in the steel business, this is the heart of where you have to be," he said. "So far the response from the mills has been very, very positive."[22]

The Porter plant was a good example of both Worthington's past and its promising future. At a cost of more than $30 million, the facility was the first of Worthington's 27-plant, 10-state operation to combine major processing and pickling capabilities under one roof, and it was Worthington's

Left: John H. McConnell, left, and Indiana Lt. Gov. Frank O'Bannon, right, cut the ceremonial ribbon at the company's new Porter, Indiana, plant.

Below: Designed to replace Worthington Steel–Chicago, the Porter plant combined pickling and processing under one roof. The huge new facility opened for operation in 1990.

single largest capital expenditure up to that time.[23] Worthington Steel–Chicago had employed 80 people at an 85,000-square-foot facility; when completed, Porter housed more than 250 workers in 450,000 square feet.[24]

Furthermore, the plant became an important toll processor for the steel mills in the Indiana Harbor area. "We upgraded all of our slitters," Ed Ferkany said of the move to Porter. "We put in a new cut-to-length line. We put in high-speed pickling. We had the temper mill in-line, at the end of the line."[25]

Porter was constructed in two phases. During Phase I, cutting, slitting and rolling equipment was moved from a rented building in Franklin Park, Illinois. Some of the equipment, although decades old, was refurbished and reinstalled at the new location. Large gaps were left on the shop floor to accommodate future growth.

Most of the employees from Chicago took jobs at Porter, and many moved to the area.[26] Worthington went to great lengths to take care of the uprooted employees. "If they wanted to move their families, we gave a full moving policy to every employee," remembered Jack Graf, who was vice president of sales at Chicago and also transferred to Porter. "The company took care of the move for them."[27]

Likewise, the Chicago offices were relocated to Porter. "It was taking the old Franklin Park plant and basically moving it down and expanding it, giving it room to grow," said Stier. "The same kind of things that you used to do there, you did in Porter. We moved the offices 4th of July weekend in 1990, and we were up and running. In part, we ran two plants for awhile, back and forth.... It was kind of like two plants in one but eventually pulled the synergies together, and it became our best plant."[28]

When completed, Porter featured the world's most advanced pickling operation, along with sophisticated in-line temper rolling, slitting, cold rolling, first stage blanking and cut-to-length capabilities.[29] Despite its size, the Porter plant became a model for team efficiency.

"We cut down a lot of the distractions," Stier said.

"We let people focus on what it is they're supposed to be doing. If we're running a machine, *we take all the things that will get in our way, all the distractions, out of it and let us focus on what we're supposed to be doing."[30]*

Setting an EPA Standard

Completed in August 1991, the pickling line was equipped to handle about 500,000 tons of steel coil a year, more than 2 percent of the production from all the mills in Indiana and Chicago.[31] Because pickling lines produced hazardous waste, they were closely monitored by the Environmental Protection Agency, and Worthington ran into some trouble when the EPA discovered the pickling line had been built before final environmental approval was granted. The line was still idle, but the EPA handed down a $40,000 fine and required Worthington to complete extra environmental controls even though the plant was already one of the cleanest in the area.[32]

"By comparison with area steel mills, it will emit relatively little into the air above northwest Indiana," reported *The Gary Post-Tribune.* "It is expected to give off 25 tons a year of nitrogen oxide, according to [the Indiana Department of Environmental Management]. Emissions from one of the major steel mills come close to 100,000 tons of nitrogen oxides a year."[33]

Stier called the penalty a "tragic misunderstanding.... We filed for the permit clear back in December. We have not tried to hide this. We had filed everything we felt like we had to file. But we didn't get everything done in time and jumped the gun a tad."[34]

Worthington agreed to the EPA's terms and learned from its mistake: Porter quickly became the EPA's model for pickling pollution control technology. The EPA selected Porter as a model because of its collection system, cleanliness and overall efficiency and used the plant to establish new Maximum Achievable Control Technology for the pickling industry.[35]

In pickling operations, a solution of hydrochloric acid and water (called "pickle liquor") was used to remove scale from the steel. For most picklers, the used pickle liquor had to be hauled away as hazardous waste, but Worthington Steel–Porter reclaimed scale from the rinse water and mixed it back into the used pickle liquor to make a higher quality product, which was sold. Used pickle liquor was used to remove phosphorous from municipal waste water.

Porter's virtually sealed system also used only 20 percent of the air that traditional systems required. The air was treated using a high efficiency scrubber that removed the acid from the air by combining it with water. This mixture was later used to dilute the original acid when the pickle liquor was made. By doing so, all scrubber byproducts were used.

The steel was rinsed with water as it left the pickling operation. Part of this wastewater went back to dilute this original acid. The remaining wastewater was treated in a clarifier, then tested and dumped into the sewer system, free of harmful pollution. The scale that was clarified out of

After a controversial start, the pickling line at Porter became a model of efficiency and set the EPA standard for environmental control in the industry. The line produced hardly any waste.

the wastewater (called sludge) had additional water removed by a microfilter, and then the remaining iron-rich sludge was added back to the used pickle liquor. Except for the clarified water and a very small amount of acid leaving the scrubbers, the pickling line was virtually waste free.[36]

The sophistication of the Porter plant, in both pickling and processing, symbolized some of the changes that had come to the U.S. steel industry. In 1994, *Iron Age New Steel* analyzed the expansion of processors into areas such as pickling and cold reducing, technologies that had traditionally belonged to the integrated mills.

"For years, integrated producers have been relying on outside processors to convert large coils into the exact forms and quantities needed by customers," the magazine noted.[37] Slitting, leveling and cutting had "flowed naturally into the service center/processor orbit," but pickling and cold rolling were still integral parts of basic steelmaking.[38] Citing "the highly successful operation of Worthington Industries" as a "good view of where sheet processing stands today," the article identified two advantages the processors had

In 1990, Worthington moved into the production of laser-welded blanks through an agreement with Thyssen Stahl AG. This technique allowed several kinds of steel to be used in one blank, creating a more efficient product.

over the integrated mills: Processors were better equipped to meet even the fussiest requirements of end users, and they often did a better job than mills of delivering product to the customer on time.[39]

Laser Welding with Thyssen

In July 1990, Worthington announced another move that advanced its technology and capabilities beyond those of the traditional processor. The company had signed an agreement with Thyssen Stahl AG, a West German steel manufacturing giant, to construct and operate a pilot plant for the production of laser-welded blanks.[40] This was Worthington's second international partnership.

Through laser welding, steel shapes of differing sizes, thicknesses, grades and types could be fused at the edges into a single flat steel blank, which was then formed into a part, such as an automobile inner door, that was lighter, stronger and less costly than existing products.[41] Previous to the laser-welding technology, automakers that wanted galvanized steel at the bottom of a car door to provide rust protection but high strength steel around the window for rigidity had to use a more expensive steel with both characteristics throughout. Tailored blanks, however, combined two types of steel into a single panel.[42]

Worthington had manufactured blanks in its cylinder plants for years, but laser welding was new in the United States. Thyssen had been supplying tailor-welded blanks to Volkswagen, Audi and Daimler-Benz in West Germany, and the joint venture united Worthington's marketing know-how and existing customer base with Thyssen's manufacturing expertise.[43]

Under the terms of the agreement, Worthington supplied flat steel pieces to the plant, called TWB, which welded them together into single blanks for the automotive, appliance and other industries.[44] John H. McConnell told a *Columbus Dispatch* reporter that Worthington believed the new technology had "exceptional growth potential."[45]

The TWB plant was positioned as an extension of Worthington's toll-processing plant in Taylor, Michigan, placing it near Detroit automakers, which used tailor-welded blanks for inner door panels, frame rails, wheel houses, door rings, fenders and floor panels.[46] It was a good move; Detroit automakers were just beginning to discover the advantages of tailor-welded blanks.[47] Some industry experts predicted demand could increase fivefold to tenfold by the end of the century.[48]

The Coveted Q1: A Bright Spot in a Downturn

The acquisitions and expansion, hopeful as they were, could not prevent bad news in 1991. That year, for only the second time in 30 years, Worthington's sales did not increase. Sales declined 4 percent to $874.9 million, while earn-

Left: Executives inspect a laser-welded blank door panel. The blank was composed of several pieces of welded steel to allow for both a rust-proof bottom and a rigid window frame.

Below: The laser-welding operation was run from Worthington's Taylor, Michigan, processing plant, which benefited from its proximity to the automotive industry in Detroit.

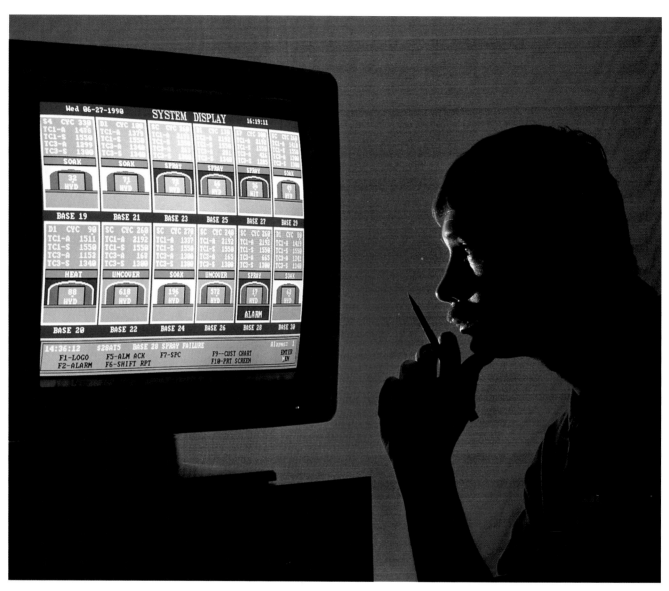

ings dropped 19 percent.[49] Processed steel sales dropped 6 percent.

There was good news mixed with the bad, however. Worthington Steel–Columbus became the first steel processor in the world to be awarded Ford Motor Company's coveted Q1 quality designation.[50] And, perhaps even more telling, in September 1991, the board of directors approved a three-for-two stock split, the first in five years and the 10th split since the company had first sold stock to the public in 1968.[51]

"We have the equipment in place and the people" to obtain record sales and profits, John H. McConnell told shareholders at the annual meeting.[52]

Worthington maintained an aggressive program of capital expansion. In the 1990s, the company enhanced its annealing capabilities with new hydrogen furnaces and the conversion of existing furnaces to the computer-controlled hydrogen atmosphere system shown here.

The Cylinder Business Rolls It Up

It was only a matter of time, he predicted, and, indeed, he was right. In 1992, business began to improve. Worthington Cylinders enjoyed an excellent year, and the division soon opened a new 140,000-square-foot plant in Jefferson,

Ohio, for the manufacture of large cylinders used to store fuel for home use in areas without access to gas lines.[53]

One month later, Worthington acquired North American Cylinders, Inc. (NACI), of Cintronelle, Alabama.[54] With 50 employees, NACI had been barely profitable, but Worthington was attracted to its product line of acetylene and other high-pressure cylinders sold to industrial gas and welding distributors.[55]

"The high-pressure compressed natural gas market is one we're staying close to so we can track it and see what's going to happen with regard to alternate fuels for motor vehicles," said Virgil Winland, vice president and general manager of all cylinder operations. "Also, as we become more environmentally conscious, chemical people are looking for reusable containers for their products. So the opportunity to grow the business is there."[56]

Worthington Cylinders was also granted ISO 9002 certifications for the Columbus and Claremore facilities. The ISO 9000 and 9002 designations, representing the approval of the International Standards Organization, were especially important to Worthington's export business, which made up about 15 percent of the cylinder division's total sales.[57] To qualify, vendors or suppliers had to maintain copious records of how their products were manufactured.

"It's all stuff that we've done very well without ISO," Winland said in *The Open Door*.

"But what ISO does is regiment you more in the area of detail. And with the complexity that has come into the business, this is really very important. Many of our overseas customers recognize ISO 9000 as being the governing body of standards on how you operate your facility.... It's a tough standard to meet, and I'm really proud of the effort our people put out to achieve this standard. Now that we can say we're ISO 9002–approved, doors open in the export business."[58]

John Christie, president of Worthington, noted how important international business was to the cylinder division. "There's growth in the domestic market in cylinders but not a lot of growth," he said. "The only way we grow is through some strategic acquisitions, but when you take our basic product here in the United States, which let's say is the 20-pound propane tank, it's a recreational item here. In other parts of the world, it's a life necessity. So the opportunities for global [growth] in the cylinders business are unbelievable."[59]

WAVE

Cylinders wasn't the only division facing great global opportunity. Worthington Industries had entered the suspended ceiling market with

In 1992, the Claremore, Oklahoma, facility earned ISO 9002 certification in recognition of its efficiency and high-quality product.

the 1984 acquisition of National Rolling Mills, the nation's third-largest manufacturer of ceiling grid. In its first six years, the business performed well, then faltered in 1991 because of the soft residential and commercial construction markets.

"In the late eighties," said Ralph Roberts, then-president of National Rolling Mills, "we started focusing on some strategic planning, and what we said is we need our businesses to be looking out and determining where the business can go in the long term. It became obvious to us at National Rolling Mills that there was consolidation occurring in the building products industry, and the first consolidation that was occurring was in the acoustical ceiling business. In order for us to benefit from that, we had to either acquire some additional companies or create some alliances."[60]

In 1991, Roberts began to pursue an opportunity that formed a joint venture with Armstrong, one of National Rolling Mills' largest customers and a competitor in suspended ceiling grid. Armstrong was also the world's largest manufac-

turer of acoustical ceiling panels. It had entered the ceiling-grid business in 1985 by acquiring a firm in Sparrows Point, Maryland, but according to Roberts, Armstrong was not completely happy with the facility.

"They were having a difficult time getting the quality Armstrong is known for," he told a reporter for *The Philadelphia Inquirer*. "They don't like products that aren't world-class."[61]

Describing Armstrong as the Coca-Cola of the building products business, Roberts said the company was looking for a way to improve its grid supply when it opened up talks with Worthington.[62]

On June 1, 1992, Worthington and Armstrong contributed their existing grid businesses to the Worthington-Armstrong Venture, called WAVE.[63] Roberts became president and created a team of managers from both companies.

"We had great expectations in early June 1992 about what we were going to do and how we were going to go out and conquer the markets,"

Right: In 1991, Worthington formed a joint venture with Armstrong called WAVE. This new business was designed to enhance Worthington's suspended ceiling grid business.

Below: In the new WAVE facility, Armstrong's expertise in acoustical tiles was married to Worthington's expertise in quality steel grid.

he recalled. "Twenty-eight days after we started our new company, we had a strike. We had an employment contract come up, and our employees walked out" at the unionized Malvern plant.[64]

A month later, with the strike finally settled, WAVE was off and running. Worthington's Malvern facility, the larger of the two original plants, manufactured grid for commercial use, while Armstrong's existing plant in Sparrows Point became the center of residential grid production.[65]

The joint venture combined Armstrong's name recognition with Worthington's manufacturing quality. Although sales for WAVE stayed flat during the recession, both companies foresaw excellent growth nationally and internationally. Soon after the joint venture was announced, WAVE pursued opportunities to expand into northeastern France and Las Vegas, Nevada.[66]

Business Picks Up

Near the end of 1992, it was clear that business was picking up for all of Worthington's divisions.[67] For the year, Worthington's sales improved 11 percent to $974.2 million, and earnings of $55.5 million were up 25 percent.[68]

At its meeting in May 1992, the board of directors elected John P. McConnell to the newly created office of vice chairman, with the responsibilities of overseeing the development of emerging business opportunities.[69] Also, Pete Klisares, a 30-year AT&T employee who retired from the telecommunications giant in 1991, became the first outside upper-level executive to join Worthington when he was named assistant to the chairman for strategic planning and the implementation of long-term objectives.[70]

"John H. McConnell originally asked me to take a look at Worthington and a strategic plan for the company," Klisares said.

"They had never really done it formally. It had always been management's vision and intuition, which is pretty remarkable in itself. I took three or four months and went through each business unit and put together a strategic plan. He then asked me to come on the board of Worthington, and finally over to Worthington full time as an assistant to the chairman."[71]

It was obvious that changes were on the horizon as the steel industry evolved and Worthington itself continued to grow and move into and out of new businesses. But the company leaders were confident they had the employees, the facilities and the products in place to resume excellent growth.

In May 1992, John P. McConnell, left, was named vice chairman of Worthington Industries. John H. McConnell, right, remained chairman and CEO.

Standing in front of a restored 1952 Oldsmobile during the company's 40th anniversary party, left to right, are Don Malenick, John H. McConnell and his son, John P. McConnell.

CHAPTER NINE

MANAGING CHANGE

1993–1995

*"Our philosophy keeps us together, solidifies us and gives continuity
to the company and its leadership."*

— John P. McConnell[1]

THE MIDDLE 1990s STARTED out great for Worthington Industries. With business strong all across America, sales were again propelled past the $1 billion mark as the company reaped rewards from the four-year, $207 million capital investment program.[2] Finally, in January 1993, Worthington was again honored as one of the 100 best companies to work for in America when authors Robert Levering and Milton Moskowitz updated their 1984 book.

"Apparently we're still doing the right things," said John H. McConnell upon hearing that his company was one of only 55 repeating from the first book.[3] Levering noted that their chosen companies "generally had someone at the helm with a vision.... They [had] a very clear idea of the workplace they want."[4]

New to the 1993 edition was Honda of America Manufacturing, based in Marysville, Ohio. Honda's vice president of administration, Don English, praised McConnell for helping Honda establish the kind of customer service and employee programs that had worked so well for Worthington. McConnell had spent time with Honda executives discussing employee programs, and Honda had modeled its profit-sharing plan after the one at Worthington.[5] "We owe a lot of what we do," English said, "to John McConnell."[6]

The Second Generation

In the midst of this good year, the company announced that 39-year-old John P. McConnell would succeed his father as CEO.[7] The senior McConnell continued as chairman of the board and maintained his office at the corporate headquarters. While the transfer of title made the changeover official, the shift in responsibility had actually begun some time earlier. John P. McConnell had been vice chairman for a year, with responsibility to oversee emerging business opportunities.[8] This forward-looking position had allowed him to be heavily involved with crucial projects such as the joint venture with Thyssen Stahl.[9]

As CEO, John P. brought to Worthington extensive experience in the company's operations. Since starting as a laborer at the Louisville plant in 1975, he had held various positions — including an eight-year stint as personnel director and positions as vice president and general manager of Worthington Steel–Columbus (the company's largest operating unit). He had been a member of the board of directors since 1990.[10] In addi-

In 1994, John H. McConnell was able to build a comprehensive medical facility at Columbus for Worthington employees.

tion to his duties at Worthington, he also spent two years outside the company as president of JMAC, Inc., the McConnell family's privately held investment company.

Yet in the midst of John P.'s training years, he almost decided against accepting his father's legacy. It was later discovered that his two-year stint at JMAC was actually a "well-orchestrated maneuver to allow him time to contemplate his future."[11] In 1995, John P. told a reporter he spent much of those two years deciding whether the career path he was on was right for him.[12] For one thing, he had "philosophical differences" with the path the company was taking by moving into areas outside its core business.[13] For another, before he stepped into his father's shoes, he wanted to make sure he could fill them. As reporter Jeff Phillips wrote for *Columbus CEO*:

> *"To his credit, John P. says, his father gave him the space he needed to work through his indecision. John P. stresses, though, that he did not return to garner his father's approval; he returned because he knew then — and knows now — that this is what he is meant to do.*
>
> *"'If I couldn't do this, I know my father would have told me so, and that's the kind of honesty I want to have with my children,' John P. reflects. 'I am confident in myself, and I know my father is confident in me.'"[14]*

Both McConnells agreed that an "evolutionary, not revolutionary" transition would be best for the company.[15] After all, John P. said, a change in leadership could be difficult for a company whose founder-chairman was synonymous with its corporate identity. And he noted that the elder McConnell would still be around "to shepherd us along."[16]

> *"Transition doesn't mean a sudden dramatic change from one thing to another. We're going to continue to do things the way we've always done them. There will be changes, there have always been changes ... [but] I know the company extremely well. I know the thoughts behind the thoughts, how it thinks and works. I've grown up with it. I'd like to continue to build what my family has started."[17]*

His father agreed. "I don't think it's that much of a transition," said John H. "I'll still be chairman of the board.... John P.'s philosophy is the same as mine. It may vary in some respects, but there's not going to be some big transitional change in the way we operate."

It quickly became apparent that father and son shared many of the same core values. Like his father, John P. was determined to visit the plants to continue the Worthington tradition of management by walking around.

"We have several options of what Worthington can be and how we can best get there," John P. wrote in the 1993 annual report.

> *"While the specifics are being developed, we see a company that is global, diversified and committed to enhancing shareholder value. We also see more and more involvement with customers — joint planning, open communications and shared risks — and it is already working for both of us. We will continue to pursue joint ventures and explore acquisitions and dispositions, with adaptability to our changing industries. We will seek to control our risk and to utilize new technologies and trends to assure competitive advantage. Above all, we will continue to follow Worthington's core philosophy of business and emphasize the role of exceptional people with a freedom to act, focused on the customer and the marketplace."[18]*

The Quality Revolution in American Industry

At the same time the younger McConnell began to assume more responsibility in running the company, American manufacturing was undergoing a profound change. Years of global competition had hurt important American industries, but that hurt carried lessons. By the early 1990s, new ideas flowed into manufacturing plants across the country. These innovative ideas were often wrapped in phrases like "total customer satisfaction," or "Just-In-Time" manufacturing or "Total Quality Management." While each of these philosophies differed in its approach, all shared the same goal: the slimming and increased efficiency of American companies to better meet global competition.

The Total Quality Management (TQM) movement, for example, began with Xerox Corporation, which had suffered major market losses to Japanese competitors in the early 1980s.[19] Like many other American companies, Xerox struggled to match the output and efficiency of Japanese companies that, shortly after the devastation of World War II, had been trained in the philosophy and principles of quality control. Interestingly, this training had come from three Americans, most notably W. Edwards Deming.[20]

When TQM began sweeping American companies, many of its principles were already in practice at Worthington: emphasis on customer satisfaction and service; commitment to quality; lean manufacturing; and empowered employees. However, as John H. McConnell observed, "The first violation occurs when you start believing that you're forever good, that you can't lose. When that violation occurs, you're on the road to decline."[21]

With this motivation in mind, in 1993 Worthington added a TQM component to its already enviable corporate style. The inspiration for the Continuous Improvement Program came after Worthington's in-house trainers attended a General Motors presentation on quality.[22]

Like other TQM movements, Worthington built its process on the belief that "every process can be measured and that old ways of doing things should be questioned to develop new efficiencies."[23] The company created problem-solving teams, and a majority of its 7,000 employees went through a three-day training program. To help further cut costs and build teamwork, each plant assembled cross-functional squads.

These teams soon identified more than 500 ways to save money. Roger Campbell, director of corporate training, told *The Columbus Dispatch* that the company was "looking for 10-cent answers to 10,000 problems."[24] The result was small, new efficiencies. For example, the company previously had wrapped coils of steel coming off the line with paper and then cut a hole in the center of the coil. One of the suggestions at the Columbus plant was to cut holes in the papers before wrapping the coils, shaving a small but valuable amount of time off the process.[25]

At Worthington, where teamwork had long been nurtured as an essential element of good business, the response to Continuous Improvement training was positive. Judi Bruce, one of the trainers, noted that while some people seemed resistant, "what really excites most employees is getting into the discussion. They feel like they are buying into the company — because it's their plant, too."[26]

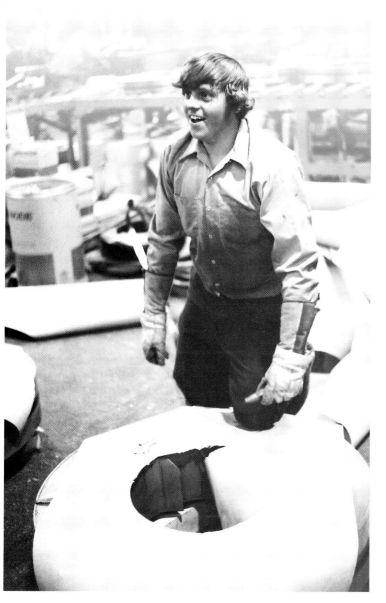

This worker is shown cutting a hole in wrapping paper after the steel has been coiled. This procedure was targeted as wasteful during the mid-1990s efficiency and quality movement.

1994: A Strong Year

This company-wide effort to cut costs and increase productivity coupled with strong demand in steel processing and pressure cylinders to give Worthington a record year in 1994: Sales reached $1.3 billion.[27]

"General economic conditions are good, and our businesses are in a great position to capitalize on the opportunity in our markets," said John P. McConnell.[28] Years of aggressive capital spending had left Worthington with more production capacity and the ability to produce superior quality.[29]

This growth, however, wasn't consistent across all the divisions. The Custom Products Division, for example, was hurt through the discontinuation of several makes of automobiles for which it supplied parts.[30] Despite the lost business, however, the division added two new plants to increase production of non-automotive products. A 120,000-square-foot facility in St. Matthews, South Carolina — the first greenfield expansion for the plastics

Right: John H. McConnell, right, pictured at a Worthington Industries annual meeting looking at products produced by the Custom Products Division, including lawn and garden equipment and a stationary infant walker.

Below: The 120,000-square-foot St. Matthews plant was the first greenfield expansion for the Custom Products Division. It began operation in 1994.

In late 1994, Worthington moved into Mexico through an agreement with Hylsa S.A. de C.V. Pictured is the galvanizing line at the plant, which was called Acerex S.A. de C.V.

group — began producing lawn and garden implements, small tools and appliances.[31] At the same time, construction began on a 170,000-square-foot facility in Lebanon, Kentucky, which became profitable only four months after starting operations.[32]

Also in 1994, Worthington's WAVE joint venture opened a plant in Valenciennes, France. This

first Worthington-run plant in Europe produced steel tracks for acoustical ceiling tiles for the European market.[33] In its first few years, WAVE enjoyed steadily advancing profits and earnings, and its growth outlook was excellent. Kenneth W.P. Hoffman, a Prudential Securities analyst, called WAVE "easily the best joint venture Worthington has ever done."[34]

Moving into Mexico

More joint ventures soon followed WAVE. In September 1994, Worthington signed an agreement with Hylsa S.A. de C.V. to operate a $24 million steel processing plant in Monterrey, Mexico, under the name Acerex S.A. de C.V. Construction began immediately on a $24 million plant.[35] The plant was designed with an annual capacity of 500,000 tons, with first-year production estimated at 240,000 tons. Through Acerex, Worthington established both a foothold in the Mexican market and a hub to serve the southwestern United States.[36]

The plant also realized a goal of John P., who had been hoping to expand Worthington into Mexico. In 1992, as vice chairman, he had spent three months exploring investment potential in Mexico.

"This isn't a south-of-the-border land of low wages," he told employees in an *Open Door* article in December 1992. "This is a country with its own special culture and history that is working hard to be successful in today's global marketplace."[37]

Like many American companies, Worthington was attracted by the opportunities created with the North American Free Trade Agreement (NAFTA) and efforts by the Mexican government to create a more stable economy. Furthermore, many Worthington customers already conducted business in Mexico. Ford had created the Mexican auto industry in 1925 when it built an assembly plant in Mexico City, and General Motors and Chrysler soon followed suit. By 1960, there were 10 assembly plants averaging 30,000 automobiles of 44 makes and 117 models annually.[38] With the rise of a middle class, the auto industry in Mexico showed growth potential in the mid-1990s.

"We are excited about getting an anchor plant from which we can grow," said John P. McConnell. "We think Mexico is an emerging market. It will also give us the opportunity to access the Southwest in the U.S.... [and] that is something we plan to build on."[39]

Worthington's Health and Wellness Center

At home, Worthington was confronting new challenges. Around this time, skyrocketing health care costs became a national concern. The Clinton administration had sought to introduce some form of national health care, but the attempt was a failure, and costs continued to climb between 12 percent and 20 percent every year. Many companies reacted to the increasingly expensive dilemma by

cutting back on health care benefits or switching to less expensive and more restrictive health management organizations, or HMOs.

Worthington, however, did the opposite. It implemented an extensive health care plan and, in June 1994, broke ground on a $2.5 million, 11,000-square-foot health and wellness center located across the pond from the corporate offices on Dearborn Drive.[40] Pete Klisares, who moved from assistant to the chairman to executive vice president in the late 1990s, said the mission of the health center was twofold: help meet the needs of employees and their families by providing "convenient, reliable, affordable" health care, and help control escalating medical expenditures by encouraging healthy living.[41]

Dr. James Mason, who had been the McConnell family's personal physician, was selected by John H. McConnell to direct the center, which featured testing facilities, including x-ray and mammography equipment, a trauma area, a laboratory and a pharmacy.

John H. McConnell had wanted to build a company-owned health facility ever since he was a salesman at Weirton Steel, which had its own small facility. McConnell and Dr. Mason had talked about the idea off and on for several years.

Dr. Mason remembered that McConnell came into his office one day in early 1993 and said, "Well, Jim, we're going to do this. We want to have a medical facility here, and would you like to be a part of it?"[42]

Mason had been a primary care physician for 35 years, but by the early 1990s the changes in the health care system had driven him to consider retirement.

"It was a time when Medicare and HMOs and managed care were taking hold," he said. "I was thinking a little bit about retiring or getting out of it because I just didn't quite enjoy it anymore.... It got to the point where you had to call somebody to ask if you could do this procedure, or the insurance company didn't like this.... I got tired of people telling me how to practice medicine."[43]

McConnell, however, gave the doctor free reign. Along with Colleen King, his nurse/business manager for 35 years, Dr. Mason hired staff and created programs. In December 1994, the center opened with three physicians, regular office hours and medical personnel on call 24 hours a day.

As a corporate health center, Worthington's was not the first, but its combination of primary care, testing capabilities and wellness programs was truly impressive. The array of services includ-

Opposite page: John H. McConnell, left, pretends to examine Dr. James Mason, right, at a Christmas party. Mason was in charge of the new medical facility at Worthington.

Above right: Pictured is the staff of the Worthington Industries medical team. From left, seated, are Colleen King, R.N., medical administrator; and Matt McHugh, M.D., primary care physician; and from left, standing, are Shirley Berrisford, receptionist; Steve Babineaux, pharmacist; Monica Verhoff, radiology technician; Carol Thompson, R.N.; James Mason, M.D., medical director; Susie Flowers, medical technician; Susie LeVine, medical secretary; Marie Gooslin, patient file administrator; and Mary Anne Sherer, R.N.

Right: A patient examining chair from the clinic.

ed free immunizations for newborns; mammography; hearing and vision screenings; classes on preventive issues such as smoking cessation and weight reduction; cholesterol and blood sugar screenings; stress tests; shots for tetanus, flu and pneumovax; lab tests; some minor surgeries such as mole removal; rehabilitation for workers injured on the job; and a drive-through and mail-order pharmacy.[44]

In addition to the three doctors, the staff included full-time and part-time nurses and a nutritionist who conducted health and wellness programs for the 2,500 Columbus-area employees. Workers at other locations were treated to traveling health fairs and preventive programs provided by nearby health professionals or organizations.[45]

"We're not there to make money," said Dr. Mason. "We try to save Worthington money. An office visit is $15. You can have 45 lab tests and it costs $10 for the whole group, and any x-rays cost $25. You could come in and have a $500 or $600 physical examination you would have on the outside with stress tests, full x-rays, laboratory work and all that, and it costs you no more than $50."[46]

In late 1994, John H. McConnell further demonstrated his commitment to the health of his community with a $7.5 million donation to a state-of-the-art heart and health center at Columbus' Riverside Methodist Hospitals.[47] The McConnell Heart/Health Center, designed by U.S. Health Corporation, pulled together a variety of prevention and rehabilitation efforts, such as exercise, nutrition and behavior modification. It was the first facility of its kind in Ohio. With his gift — to which the company later added $1 million — McConnell paid a debt of gratitude to Riverside for having saved his wife's life nine years earlier when she was diagnosed with a rare heart tumor. "I think we can help a lot of people," he said. "We want this to be first class."[48]

The Rewards of Good Business

The upswing that began in 1994 continued into the next year. In 1995, Worthington was rewarded with four consecutive quarterly records in sales and earnings. Sales for steel processing and cylinders alone were more than $1 billion, accounting for 70 percent of the company's total business. Custom products posted a 21 percent gain over the previous year's figures on sales of $302.1 million. In the cast products segment, sales increased to a record $153.1 million.[49] This was led by strong demand for freight railcars.

In 1994, the cylinder group manufactured about 11 million cylinders and, in the midst of a tremendous growth spurt, targeted South America, the Pacific Rim and the Caribbean. The division soon gained much-needed manufacturing capacity when operations began at a new $12 million, 115,000-square-foot facility in Westerville, a suburb of Columbus.[50]

Jim Knox, plant manager, estimated the plant would add another $80 million in sales for the division, which already contributed $180 million in annual sales. "Because of our growth and the doubling of sales in the last three years, we had no place to spread out equipment" at the Columbus facility, said Knox.[51]

The plant featured a new, EPA-friendly powder painting system to eliminate waste. "What drops on the floor is reused," said Knox.[52] Although 30 percent less labor was needed, workers at the plant were able to make 4,000 cylinders in an eight-hour shift, compared with 2,400 at the Dearborn Drive facility.[53]

Worthington Machine Technology

That same year, Capital Die, Tool and Machinery — the company's engineering and machine shop — changed its name to Worthington Machine Technology to reflect its expanding opportunities. Capital Die had been founded in 1916 near downtown Columbus and operated under private ownership until 1980, when Worthington, then one of its largest customers, saw the need for experienced, in-house expertise to support its growing steel and cylinder businesses. In 1983, Capital's tool and die makers, machinists and fitters relocated to Worthington's industrial complex.[54]

As Worthington Machine Technology (WMT), the segment continued to manufacture custom machines, dies, tools and fixtures and provide machine repair. WMT allowed Worthington's business units to realize significant cost savings. In 1995, "bottom-line savings to Worthington operations [totaled] more than $1 million," noted Bruce Ruhl, who was named general manager of WMT. "Because of the associated benefits, we encourage all Worthington operating units to use the service to help reduce expenses."[55]

Although 60 percent of WMT's sales came from servicing Worthington's own business units, it also served outside customers.[56] WMT designed and built machinery for automated assembly, materials handling, assembly, welding and testing applications.

A Growing Infrastructure

As the company continued to grow, Worthington began to confront the challenges of growth — an issue that would become more pressing with time. First, however, Worthington began to restructure its information-processing needs and establish an enterprise-wide information system.

Traditionally, the company had three distinct divisions in its information system — mainframe operations, factory floor engineering systems and personal computers. "In many cases these units did not talk to each other, resulting in islands of technology that were not compatible," said Bill Miller, management information systems manager.[57]

The systems group brought the three parts of the information system together by creating a corporate infrastructure that allowed for a seamless transfer of information not only within individual business units but throughout the corporation. For these efforts, Worthington was the only Columbus-area firm to be recognized in *Computerworld* magazine's October 9, 1995, listing of the companies best at deploying information technology.[58] Each firm on the "Premier 100" list was chosen on the basis of productivity.

Almost a Minimill

Although the mid-1990s was a time of tight supply in the steel industry, Worthington kept a steady supply of steel through its agreement with Rouge Steel, which supplied a stream of high-quality steel at competitive prices.[59] But the Rouge partnership could not guarantee supply for future growth. "Unless you have some real friends in the marketplace," John H. McConnell remarked, "you're hurting for steel."[60]

In 1995, Worthington processed about 3 million tons of steel, and company projections indicated that the figure could double within three to five years. Looking for ways to ensure a steady supply of raw material, the company considered what some analysts viewed as a radical option. It was one that would have changed the nature of Worthington Industries.[61]

Worthington made plans to build a minimill.

Rumors whirled through the steel industry for some time before John H. McConnell, speaking to shareholders in late 1994, confirmed that his company had tentative plans to build a minimill — at a cost of $500 million to $600 million — that could employ up to 400 people at a "site yet to be determined."[62] McConnell told a *Columbus Dispatch* reporter that the list of possible sites had been shortened to "four or five," including locations in western Ohio, Indiana and

Kentucky, and the new mill would employ an electric arc furnace. The mill would produce an estimated 2.6 million tons of steel per year, primarily for Worthington's use.[63]

The industry was rife with speculation that the fastest-growing processor in the nation was about to become a steel producer. Some financial analysts weighed in on the negative side. In a March 18, 1995, article, *Financial World* opined that the cost would be exorbitant— "especially for a steel processor that depends on a low cost-structure to insulate itself from price fluctuations" — and urged Worthington to find another way to solve its supply problem.[64]

Characteristically, the company considered its options carefully. In November 1994, the *Courier-Journal* in Louisville, Kentucky, reported that Worthington would place a mill in either Findlay, Ohio; Hancock County, Kentucky; or Spencer County, Indiana.[65] The company refused to confirm the report but said it was involved in a process that included finding a site, analyzing the possibility of a partnership and assessing potential vendors. "We have absolutely no parameters on the timing of the announcement," a company spokesperson said. "We want to take a full look at all aspects of the minimill project."[66]

Furthermore, talks about a joint venture with U.S. Steel were broken off. Charles Bradford, an analyst with USB Securities who followed Worthington, said that U.S. Steel was committed to making a lower-grade product than Worthington wanted, thus ending a two-year negotiating process.[67]

To Delta Instead

By the next spring, Worthington had decided not to go ahead with plans to build its own mill. "We looked the devil in the eye and retreated on that," John P. McConnell told *Financial World*.[68] Instead, the company announced it would build a $65 million steel-processing facility to serve a minimill being constructed by North Star/BHP Steel in Delta, Ohio, just west of Toledo. The mill represented a 50/50 venture by North Star Steel, headquartered in Minneapolis and the eighth-largest U.S. steel company, and Australian-based BHP, the world's 13th-largest steel producer.[69]

John H. McConnell posing next to the restored 1952 Oldsmobile given to him by Worthington employees. This car was a replica of the one that McConnell borrowed money against to start Worthington Industries.

The Delta processing plant represented Worthington's largest steel processing center to date. It was expected to bring in more than $250 million in annual sales for Worthington and was part of a "broader agreement" with North Star/BHP.

"We've reached a long-term supply agreement for about one-third of the mill's annual output," said John H. McConnell. "We intend to keep the agreement flexible in terms of tonnage and mix to maximize the benefit to each of us."[70]

The decision against becoming a steel producer did not represent a change in the compa-ny's strategy since the original impetus be-hind building a minimill was to gain an "assured source" of steel.[71]

"We became convinced that, for the next three to five years, we could secure our incremental raw material steel supply on favorable terms to achieve our growth objectives without having to build a minimill," McConnell told *Metal/Center News*, adding that this supply deal represented "new tons on top of what we're currently buying."[72]

"Worthington has solved its need for a stable supplier," wrote a pleased *Financial World*, "while saving itself about $500 million in capital. And it doesn't have to worry about competing in the crowded hot rolled steel market."[73]

McConnell Honored at Home

In August 1995, the employees of Worthington Industries presented their company's founder with a fountain for the pond at corporate headquarters.[74] The gift was in celebration of 40 years of sustained growth since John H. McConnell first put up his 3-year-old car as collateral for the loan with which he founded the steel processing industry.

With net sales nearing $1.5 billion, Worthington celebrated 1995 as another remarkable year in four remarkable decades.[75] In 1955, The Worthington Steel Company had incorporated with five employees, sales of $350,000 and $14,000 in profits.[76] "Today," wrote Don Malenick in *The Open Door*, "our sales are $6 million per day — 17 times our first year of sales."[77]

As the 1995 annual report stated, the company had made it happen by putting customers first:

"The genesis of Worthington Industries was the idea of creating a new kind of steel service business — one that would meet customer needs for more specialized orders, shorter lead times and improved quality. By performing services more efficiently and creating new products, the company has helped customers reduce costs and focus on core elements of their own businesses. In short, the company was created to serve the customer."[78]

Perhaps most impressively, the company had sustained consistent growth figures in a cyclical industry. Between 1955 and 1995, Worthington Industries had established sales records in all but three of its 40 years, and record earnings in 36 of those years. Since Worthington's IPO in 1968, the average annual rate of growth in earnings per share was 22 percent, fulfilling John H. McConnell's goal.[79]

With dividends reinvested, a $750 investment in Worthington Industries when it went public in 1968 would have swelled to $265,247 as of May 31, 1995.[80]

In 1996, Worthington purchased Dietrich Industries, part of a strategy designed to move the company into residential steel framing.

CHAPTER TEN

BACK TO THE FUTURE

1996–PRESENT

"We treat our customers, employees, investors and suppliers as we would like to be treated."

— Worthington's Golden Rule

IN 1995, WORTHINGTON INDUSTRIES enjoyed the best year in its history. John H. McConnell's basement business had grown into a $1.5 billion company with 55 facilities in 21 states and, by year's end, five countries, including China.[1] As the country's leading intermediate processor of flat rolled steel, Worthington processed more than 3 million tons of steel annually for more than 1,700 customers.[2]

Although it was the nation's largest steel processor, Worthington accounted for only 7 percent of the processing and distributing market.[3] The company's growing sales were also derived from a range of other businesses, including the manufacture of pressure cylinders, suspended ceiling grid, custom plastics, precision metals and steel castings.

As Worthington officers often pointed out, none of its businesses were the high-profile kind that usually attracted national attention. And yet Worthington was a nationally known company with an unblemished record of excellence to its employees, shareholders and customers. The culture that enabled this success was based on Worthington's very simple golden rule: Treat your customers, employees, investors and suppliers the way you would want to be treated.

Flexibility and adaptability were also encouraged at Worthington, from the shop floor to the executive suite. In the late 1990s, this flexibility would once again be called upon during a time of reassessment, reorganization and strategic planning. But this was a necessary upheaval. After the record-setting sales of 1995, revenues in 1996 stayed flat at $1.47 billion while net earnings fell 22 percent. A mild softening in the economy had reduced both the demand for and the price of steel products. Profit was also affected by a General Motors strike and the temporary shutdown of a zinc-plating line at the Malvern plant.[4]

As its profit dropped, Worthington found itself in the unfamiliar position of having to convince Wall Street it was a good investment. Even in 1995, despite the company's impressive performance, Worthington stock posted a below-market-average return of 6 percent. At the September annual meeting, John H. McConnell told shareholders that company stock was dragged down because the entire steel industry was out of favor.

"We can't do much about it except to put good numbers on the table," he said. "It's across the board. Investors in New York don't seem to care

Pictured accepting the Horatio Alger Award, John H. McConnell had grown his company into a $1.5 billion corporation and the nation's premier steel processor by 1996.

about steel right now. But it will come back up.... I've never been more confident in this company in 40 years."[5]

A March 1996 issue of *Financial World* pointed out that "rock-bottom valuations [were] typical of the processor group."[6] Even so, *Financial World* writer John Geer saw Worthington as a good opportunity for investors, with opportunity for growth that was the best it had been in five years:

> *"Many smaller processors are struggling because they haven't been able to keep up with the demanding specs manufacturers require. Also, the car companies want only a handful of suppliers, which should accelerate the carnage. Half of the 7,000 U.S. steel processors and distributors in business in 1980 are gone. And Kenneth Hoffman of Prudential Securities expects the remaining number to dwindle to 750 by 2005. So top-tier processors can pick up market share from attrition or through cheap acquisitions."[7]*

Howard Rudnitsky, writing for *Forbes*, agreed. "Big as it is," he noted, Worthington did not "plan to rest on past laurels.... So, over the next two years, Worthington will probably double capital spending, to about $150 million a year from $61 million currently, to build new plants and to acquire existing ones.... Count on this company to grow smartly."[8]

Almost immediately, Worthington bore this prediction out and dramatically increased capital spending. The budget swelled to $109 million in 1996 and would almost triple by 1998.[9] A clean balance sheet — partially a result of the decision not to build a minimill — allowed Worthington to lavish capital on both greenfield sites and acquisitions.

"We really hadn't spent much money for probably 13 years," said John P. McConnell. "We had really been spending just around maintenance levels for quite a while.... It was time to get off the stick and get moving."[10]

The Dietrich Acquisition

Within weeks of the *Forbes* article, Worthington announced its single largest acquisition to date, the $176 million purchase of Pittsburgh-based Dietrich Industries.[11] With annual sales of $285 million, Dietrich was the country's largest producer of galvanized metal framing products for commercial and residential construction.[12]

It was a market *Financial World* called "potentially explosive."[13] Steel had already built the United States' landmark skyscrapers and bridges, but only recently had residential builders begun turning to steel frames. Home builders liked steel's strength, durability and recyclability and were tired of lumber's inconsistent prices and quality. The American Iron & Steel Institute called steel the "future" of residential construction and listed four reasons:

> *"1. Houses framed with steel are more resistant to disasters such as fire, hurricanes and earthquakes, as well as straighter and stronger;*
> *"2. The steel from six recycled cars can frame a house that would require the timber from 40 trees;*
> *"3. Because steel framing stays straight and true, it helps prevent air leaks that result in costly loss of energy [for homeowners]; and*
> *"4. According to a recently released study commissioned by EarthKind and conducted by Baylor University, steel framing should be recognized as a 'green' building material based on economic and environmental criteria."[14]*

Founded in 1959, Dietrich at the time of its acquisition employed 1,500 people at 18 facilities in 15 states. The company produced more than 35 percent of the metal framing used in the domestic residential and commercial building industries, and it was the only metal framing manufacturer with national distribution. In addition to framing, Dietrich also produced stainless steel blanks and a complete line of roll-formed garage-door sections. At the time of the acquisition, Dietrich was completing a period of heavy capital investment, having spent more than $100 million on modern equipment and facilities over the previous five years.[15]

Because it was a healthy company and fairly large already, the news of the acquisition "really rattled the foundations" at Dietrich, remembered Ed Ponko, Dietrich executive vice president. "But I can say that Worthington really went out of its way

to make us feel like part of a family," he added. "We liked its golden rule and its business tenets."[16]

In fact, Worthington's reputation was a major reason Dietrich officers supported the acquisition. Like Worthington, Dietrich was a family-run company with a history of employee-friendly policies and some of the same business philosophies that had made Worthington so successful. William Dietrich had taken over his family business from his father and was looking for a buyer who would keep the company name and quality reputation.

"He had heard we were looking around in the [metal framing] market," remembered John P. McConnell.

"He was in his late fifties and ... didn't have any family that was going to take over the business.... That's one thing that time and time again, when you talk about the philosophy and the reputation of [Worthington Industries] for treating people well, has been like a magnet for bringing

Steel framing had long been a favorite of commercial builders and began to find application in the residential construction market in the late 1990s. Worthington's 1996 Dietrich acquisition, its largest to date, was expected to expand this business.

good companies run by [good] people here. When they're ready to end the family reign or they're going to exit the business, they'd like to sell to somebody like us. It's always given us a good first look at an awful lot of companies."[17]

Following the acquisition, Dietrich kept its name, its headquarters in Pittsburgh and William Dietrich as CEO — as well as cherished projects. "One of the first questions I asked Bill Dietrich after he told me he sold the company to Worthington was whether he told them about the Infinity project we're working on," Ponko said.

"This was near and dear to our hearts and has a lot of long-term ramifications and a lot of cash up front with very little in deliverables for several years. He had indicated that he had and that Worthington was fully on board with that. That struck me as really unusual for a large company, and that was the biggest step for me right off the bat."[18]

Worthington, meanwhile, gained a tremendous opportunity. "If anyone doubted that we are a growth company, this is a signal that we are going to do the things we said we were going to do," said John P. McConnell.[19] "The acquisition should make some sense to the market. It makes sense to us."[20]

SCM Technologies Acquisition

Growth company indeed. Six months later, in June 1996, Worthington expanded its global gas cylinder operation with the acquisition of a Canadian cylinder maker, SCM Technologies.[21] Based in Tilbury, Ontario, SCM employed 100 people and had achieved annual sales of $10

million by designing, engineering and manufacturing high-pressure industrial, medical, Halon and electronic gas cylinders.[22]

Although most of the company's products were shipped to the United States, SCM conducted significant business in Canada and Great Britain. Virgil Winland, group vice president of Worthington Cylinders, explained the acquisition's benefit.

"This strategic acquisition significantly increases our presence in the high-pressure cylinder market and strengthens our position as North America's premier cylinder producer. SCM is in the process of introducing a number of new products that will further enhance the profitability of an already solid product line."[23]

The Joint Ventures Pay Off

Throughout 1996, Worthington also enjoyed the continuing success of its joint ventures. The Worthington-Armstrong Venture (WAVE) posted a double-digit increase in earnings as it continued to gain domestic and worldwide market share. The opening of a facility in Las Vegas in early 1996 strengthened WAVE's presence in the growing Western market, and in 1997, the venture launched a new plant in China, acquired an

---

In 1997, WAVE launched a facility in China. John P. McConnell greets Chinese dignitaries during a plant tour of the Columbus processing facility.

existing facility in Spain and announced new green-field operations for England and Benton Harbor, Michigan.[24] Around this time, Ralph Roberts left WAVE to go back to Worthington, and Stephen Senkowski came from Armstrong to head the successful joint venture.

"There is a mix of Armstrong and Worthington people here," Senkowski said of WAVE. "We're a very global business, and as we grow, our opportunity has grown."[25]

In that same busy year, Worthington Specialty Processing, the joint venture with USX, opened up new markets with a blanking press. The new TWB laser welding facility also became fully operational and, due to a rapid increase in the use of laser-welded blanks in the auto industry, was expanded.[26]

The End of an Era

Over the years, much of Worthington's success had been attributed to John H. McConnell. He had been responsible for creating the environment that allowed Worthington's employees to excel in their positions and their work. With such an impressive legacy at his company, there would probably never be a good time for him to retire — but with a new generation of leaders moving up and his son fully prepared to lead the company, the 73-year-old McConnell was ready to step back.

On September 19, 1996, the founder of Worthington Industries formally relinquished his title. "It was my idea," he said. "The board didn't bring it up. But I'm not exactly riding into the sunset. I'll be around. The company will go on as it has in the past."[27]

The emotional announcement was made at the annual shareholders meeting. John P. was named chairman of the board in addition to his duties as CEO and vowed to carry on the family tradition. In making the announcement, John P. McConnell told shareholders, "This is John H. McConnell's philosophy. And as long as it is here, he is here."[28] His father was given the title of chairman emeritus and retained his positions as a director and chairman of the executive committee.[29]

An article in the September 29, 1996, *Columbus Dispatch* paid tribute to the outgoing chairman as a savvy entrepreneur and a sharer of wealth:

Already CEO, John P. McConnell was named chairman of the board when his father stepped down in 1996. Both father and son expected a smooth transition.

"[Mark] Koprucki, an analyst for The Ohio Company, said Worthington's record of profitability is 'astounding.'

"'It's one of the most consistently profitable steel companies in existence, one of the few that has essentially ignored economic downturns,' he said....

"[Don] Malenick said downturns weren't really ignored. Instead of cutting back like most companies, investment was increased to prepare for the economic rebound and accelerated growth. The only layoff Worthington ever had came in the early 1960s, when several employees were out of work for two weeks....

Over the course of his long career with Worthington, John H. McConnell emerged as a legend in manufacturing and steel processing, and he continued to represent the company to the outside world. He is pictured, clockwise from left, with Gen. Colin
Powell during a CEO roundtable, at a prayer breakfast sponsored by Worthington Industries featuring speaker Elizabeth Dole,
and with former Vice President Dan Quayle and John P. McConnell.

*"'We had no job descriptions,' said Malenick.
'People were encouraged to get involved, to grow
in the job and grow the company.'"[30]*

As chairman and founder of Worthington
Industries, John H. McConnell reaped accolades,
including the Horatio Alger Award, the Ohio
Governor's Award, the title Entrepreneur of the
Year and the Outstanding Chief Executive
Award.[31] As chairman emeritus and an entrepre-
neurial legend, he continued to earn honors. In
October 1998 he was inducted into the Columbus
Hall of Fame, joining such figures as World War I
flying ace Eddie Rickenbacker, writer-cartoonist
James Thurber and Wendy's restaurant-chain
founder Dave Thomas.[32]

"There are those people that are just a little bit
golden for some reason, and John H. McConnell is
one of those people," said Pete Klisares, who joined
Worthington's board of directors in 1991, then
became assistant to John H. McConnell.

*"Because of the kind of person he is and
his integrity and character and openness, he
engenders that in other people. He always
had a great instinct about doing things or
not doing things, or believing in things when
other people might not. He came from bolting
the machine down on the floor himself and
running it to the point where most of the
employees here will do anything in the world
for him because they trust him that much.*

They trust his fairness. They trust his judgment and integrity."[33]

Soon after his announcement, McConnell flew to New York with his son and other members of the company management to accept the National Football Foundation and College Hall of Fame Gold Medal Award, the highest honor given by the organizations to college athletes who distinguish themselves in their chosen field.[34] In accepting the award, McConnell added his name to an exclusive list that includes five U.S. presidents — George H. W. Bush, Gerald Ford, Richard Nixon, John F. Kennedy and Dwight D. Eisenhower — as well as such luminaries as Gen. Douglas MacArthur, Gen. Norman Schwarzkopf, former congressman Jack Kemp and baseball great Jackie Robinson.[35]

The Gerstenslager Story

As the elder McConnell stepped back, his company continued expanding under the direction of John P. McConnell. In December 1996, Worthington announced the acquisition of Plastics Manufacturing, Inc. (PMI), a producer of injection-molded and thermoformed plastic parts primarily for the business equipment, commercial airline and medical industries.[36] Located in Harrisburg, North Carolina, PMI enhanced the custom plastics group, opened new markets and added $80 million in annual sales.[37]

A few months later, Worthington announced another acquisition, this one designed to augment the steel processing division. In February 1997, Worthington purchased The Gerstenslager Company, the nation's leading independent supplier of body panels for the automotive and commercial truck industries. Based in Wooster, Ohio,

Through its various businesses, Worthington Industries supplied many components for automobile dashboards, including the plastic molded parts and metal components.

Gerstenslager stamped, assembled, primed, packaged and shipped components such as fenders, doors and hoods for OEM service parts distributors and automotive dealers.[38]

Worthington paid approximately $113 million in stock for Gerstenslager, which had been owned by JMAC (the McConnell family's investment company) since 1980.[39] At the time of the acquisition, Gerstenslager was run by Jay Wisner, a former General Motors manufacturing executive who had been recruited out of retirement by John H. McConnell in 1984.

Ken Vagnini, who had worked for Gerstenslager since 1978, remembered the excitement when he found out that Gerstenslager was being purchased by JMAC. (Incidentally, it was JMAC's first acquisition.)

"It was exciting," Vagnini said. "I thought it would give us the financial platform that the company needed. When Mr. John H. McConnell saw

Workers at The Gerstenslager Company, which had stamping and fabrication divisions geared to the automobile industry. Worthington purchased Gerstenslager in 1997.

us, he envisioned the growth potential, so when we started developing and formalizing our culture, we used the Worthington philosophy as our guide."[40]

At the time, Gerstenslager had only about $15 million in sales, but JMAC invested heavily, and the company began to grow under Wisner's direction. By the late 1990s, with $120 million in sales, Gerstenslager had outgrown the investment company, according to John Christie, then president of JMAC. Gerstenslager was "a much better fit for a company with the financial resources to exploit its strong growth potential," he said.[41]

Gerstenslager added a rich history to the Worthington story. Founded in 1860 as a carriage factory in the rural town of Marshallville, Ohio, the company produced buggies, surreys and wagons until 1907, when, in need of a larger building and a location closer to shipping centers, it relocated to the north-central Ohio town of Wooster. In the early 1920s, Gerstenslager changed its production facilities to make van bodies and special truck bodies. Following World War II, the company produced vehicles for fire departments, libraries, hospitals, dental units, canteens, mobile x-ray units and television units for all the major networks. In the early 1950s, Gerstenslager built mail trucks and other vehicles for the U.S. Postal Service. Its stamping and fabrication divisions were put in place during the 1960s, when the company began producing parts for the automotive, truck and agricultural industries.[42]

Since its acquisition by JMAC in 1980, Gerstenslager had compiled an impressive list of quality awards and designations, including the Ford Q1 rating, Targets for Excellence from General Motors and Quality of Excellence from Chrysler. At the time of the acquisition, it was also in the process of attaining QS9000 certification.[43]

Culturally, the company was already very close to Worthington, and when Wisner retired in 1999, Vagnini was named president of Gerstenslager.

John Christie, who in 1999 moved from JMAC to become Worthington's president and chief operating officer, said JMAC was able to help Worthington by developing promising businesses like Gerstenslager, and even to help Worthington's hometown city of Columbus.[44] In 1997, JMAC invested in the Bluejackets, a Columbus-based National Hockey League expansion team.

Through its laser welding joint venture, TWB Company, Worthington was able to offer a more cost-efficient blank for automobile doors. Laser welding enabled Worthington to join several pieces of steel with different characteristics into one smooth piece.

"That was a major commitment that John H. McConnell made to this community," said Christie. "He has the idea that he owes this community for the success he's had, and he thinks if this community is going to be a 21st century community, it needs professional sports, and he was willing to sign up."[45]

A Million Tons a Year

In March 1997, Worthington broke ground in Decatur, Alabama, for a new, 750,000-square-foot steel processing plant adjacent to a Trico Steel minimill.[46] The 1997 annual report promised shareholders that the Decatur mill would be something special.

"Strategically located in the heart of the country's fastest growing steel market, this facility will be the premier intermediate steel processing operation in the country. Pickling and slitting will start up during the first half of calendar 1998, while cold rolling will be phased in approximately one year later. Upon completion, Decatur will be Worthington's largest steel facility, with the capacity to process more than one million tons of steel per year."[47]

Twelve months later, the Decatur plant began limited operations. The centerpiece of the facility was a 1-million-ton, 72-inch-wide cold roll tandem mill that, with accompanying annealing and temper-rolling capabilities, began running during the summer of 1998, about nine months ahead of schedule.[48]

"It's our largest facility to date," said Harold "Butch" Dell, who was part of the operating team that opened Decatur. "Its business plan is to be the largest single facility in our business group, and it's designed and laid out as one of the most efficient cold roll sheet-processing facilities, either in the country or in the world. A lot of the technology we have in this plant is in use in most of the modern mills today."[49]

Together, Delta and Decatur, when fully operational, had the capacity to produce more than $700 million in revenues.[50]

A Hallmark of Teamwork

On August 14, 1997, as Worthington celebrated the opening of its second huge plant and a string of successful acquisitions, a group of plant managers gathered in downtown Columbus for a dinner that none of them would forget. After a managers' meeting that day, the group headed out to a local restaurant. James Ballard, the plant manager of Monroe, Ohio, was present and remembered when Ralph Roberts joined the group.

"He introduced himself and shook everybody's hand, then sat down at the table and said, 'Boy, it's a shame about Monroe.' Everybody kind of looked at me, and I said, 'What's wrong with Monroe?' He said, 'Oh, for heaven's sake, Jim, you need to go to Monroe. Your plant is on fire.'

"We thought he was joking, but Ralph kind of lost color in his face. He turned white and he said, 'No, Jim, I'm telling you the truth; you need to go now. Your people in Monroe are going to need you.'"[51]

Roberts hadn't been joking, and Ballard sped back to Monroe to find the street blocked off and reporters milling around as the plant burned in the distance. "The first thing I wanted to do was find out if there were any injuries," Ballard remembered. "I talked to Mike Albers, who was plant superintendent, and several maintenance people and found out there were no injuries. That was outstanding, and that was my main concern. After that, we wanted to assess the damage."[52]

Before the flames could be extinguished, the facility was nearly destroyed. The pickling capabilities were demolished, and the slitting and blanking operations were severely damaged.

"It was almost like a death in the family," recalled corporate trainer Mary Wood-Anderson. "People walked around like zombies. We felt it all through the company."[53]

The fire had a profound impact on Worthington and proved a valuable test of the company's compassion for its employees and its dedication to its customers. When Ballard arrived on the scene that first night, a reporter asked him a leading question about the "350 people that worked there." Ballard first joked with the media crews to lighten the mood, then, before confirming his answer with any other executives, said, "Worthington has always been good to its people, and I'm sure this will be no different."[54]

The next day, the senior management team began to arrive in Monroe and set up a "war room" to deal with the crisis. All the hourly workers were told to stay home for the day and were guaranteed their wages would continue. The next step involved the customers supplied by Monroe. Materials-handling people were called back to the burned plant to remove any salvageable steel. To fill orders, more steel would have to come from somewhere else.

"That facility was the single largest supplier to a General Motors facility in Dayton, Ohio," recalled Jack Graf, who headed sales at the Porter, Indiana, plant.

"When Monroe burned, Worthington had material shipped from Monroe, Ohio, to Porter, Indiana, on Saturday. The Porter employees had the

In 1997, John P. McConnell was presented with the seal of the state of Alabama after announcing plans to build a new, 750,000-square-foot steel processing plant in Decatur.

material processed, pickled, slit, packaged and shipped to the customer by Monday morning. The customer could not believe that Worthington employees would do what they did."[55]

With the immediate crisis taken care of, Worthington turned its attention to the long-term future of the Monroe employees. Had they worked for another company, these workers might naturally have assumed they were out of a job or could have expected to be laid off at least until the plant was rebuilt. Worthington, however, offered the Monroe employees positions at other company facilities while the plant was being rebuilt.

"We told the employees that we needed them," Ballard said.

"We still wanted them but to be able to maintain the business, we needed them to go to different facilities. Nobody likes being asked to leave home, but they all understood, and they all knew the importance of satisfying the customers' needs. We gave the employees each a packet and a $200 cash advance so they wouldn't be out of

On August 14, 1997, much of Worthington's Monroe plant was destroyed by fire. This photo was taken shortly after the blaze. Although the plant was almost gutted, no one was hurt, and Worthington was still able to fill its customers' orders without any delay by sending material to the Porter facility. No Worthington workers lost their jobs as a result of the fire.

pocket money. We leased cars and apartments. It was a very difficult time for me, but I think the response was great. I think there are very few companies in today's world that are going to have the president of the corporation at that site the very next day."[56]

Within seven months, every Monroe employee was back in town, and the rebuilt facility was beginning limited operations. Within 13 months, the new Monroe facility produced its first salable pickled coil. The new pickling operation featured an in-line temper mill and a capacity 50 percent greater than the two lines it replaced.[57]

"There's a lot of companies today that brag about having great people and how well they treat their people, but they never have gone through this kind of test to see how they're going to react," Ballard said.

"Everybody, when that fire occurred, was wondering if Worthington was just going to shut the doors and bulldoze the property and rebuild somewhere else. But corporate was very, very quick to react. They let us know Monroe has always been a great location and they needed us. That was absolutely critical, and the employees got to see that Worthington really stands behind its philosophy."[58]

In January, this kind of dedication to its employees earned Worthington a place on *Fortune* magazine's debut list of the "The 100 Best Companies to Work for in America."[59] Worthington was chosen from more than 1,000 companies that were at least 10 years old and had a minimum of 500 employees.[60] Reporters Robert Levering and Milton Moskowitz found that Worthington's rate of voluntary turnover was only 4 percent, among the lowest in the surveyed companies. The authors also cited the company's no-layoff policy, employee councils,

THE WINNING WAY

THE RAPID SUCCESS OF WORTHINGTON Industries has resulted largely from the company's commitment to provide total solutions for its customers: Worthington doesn't sell just steel — it sells steel solutions.

Employees in each department are charged with the responsibility to fill customers' needs, and they use an impressive level of teamwork to achieve that goal. "They stand behind their product," said Joe Szuba, principal research scientist associate at Ford Motor Company. "They have a 'locker-room environment' at Worthington Steel, meaning they look out for each other and they look out for their customers. It's really something."

Joe Szuba knows. As the supervisor of clutches and torque converters at Ford in the early 1980s, he worked closely with Worthington on a project that eventually helped save Ford Motor Company, which had been teetering "on the brink" of disaster. In the early 1980s, the once mighty car maker was being beaten by leaner Japanese companies.

"We were losing something like $750 million each quarter," Szuba recalled, "and we were selling assets just to make payroll." Part of the problem was that, along with the other domestic automakers, the archetype of the American auto industry was out of touch with what the public wanted. The popularity of

fuel-efficient compacts was growing, but Ford's drawing boards were still filled with large, rear-wheel-drive gas guzzlers. The company needed a breakthrough product — and needed it fast.

Ford engineers began working on a roomy sedan that would offer more comfort than Japanese competitors could but would provide a similar level of fuel efficiency and overall reliability. The model name? The Ford Taurus.

Designing was one thing; building it was a different story. To achieve better fuel efficiency, Ford needed to remove weight from the sedan without sacrificing size and comfort. At the time, sedans were equipped with heavy (and often unreliable) cast-iron clutch cylinders. When Ford put out the order for a clutch cylinder that would require a lighter, stronger steel, the company discovered that few steel companies were willing to try; because of the small volume involved in making a prototype, the integrated steel mills couldn't afford to work with the automaker. "I called U.S. Steel a couple of times," Szuba remembered, "but never got anyone to show up."

While Szuba tried to get an audience with the integrated mills, he was called on by a Worthington salesperson, Ron Maciejowski (now vice president, business strategy and profit sharing accounts and medical clinic (which had served more than 14,000 patients in 1996) as factors that made it a "Great Place to Work."[61]

Growth Abroad

By 1998, the cylinder division accounted for 15 percent, or roughly $300 million, of the company's annual revenues and was looking for additional growth opportunities.[62] The division had recently begun a joint venture with a propane tank manufacturing plant in Brazil. The new company, Worthington S.A., made partners of Worthington and three of Brazil's leading gas distributors in the production of cylinders at a plant in Sao Paulo. It was Worthington's first direct investment in South America.

"We're getting a foothold down there," said Winland. "The cylinder market is huge. We bought this to take sales significantly higher than $20 million."[63]

At the time, CEO John P. McConnell agreed. "Manufacturing outside the United States provides great avenues of future growth for our cylinder

---

flat roll products). At the time, Worthington was a $500 million company, and Szuba was a bit skeptical. But Maciejowski soon impressed him with an extraordinary level of knowledge; like all salespeople at Worthington Steel, he'd spent six months working in a processing plant and had taken a company course entitled "Metallurgy for the Non-Metallurgist."

Next, Maciejowski brought in Ted Armbruster, a metallurgist from Worthington's technical services department. Initially, Ford's engineers wanted an exotic, high-strength steel, but Armbruster believed such a high-cost material was unnecessary. "Our customers are experts at what they do," noted Ted Armbruster, "but they don't know steel. We know steel."

Throughout the project, the technical services department produced several iterations of a clutch cylinder, tinkering with the steel until it met the carmaker's specifications for both strength and lightness. Worthington came up with a sheet metal clutch cylinder that performed beautifully. Moreover, the clutch cylinder was produced at a cost of five dollars less per part than Ford had been paying. At three parts per car, it saved Ford millions.

Over the course of the next decade and a half, that figure would reach into the hundreds of millions. The sheet metal clutch cylinder not only became a key component of the wildly popular Taurus, which has been called "the car that saved Ford Motor Company," but also was incorporated into the automaker's other domestically produced automatic transmissions and later copied by other car companies. Once, when Ford had a problem with a metal part obtained from a different supplier, Worthington sent an engineer up from Columbus to find out what was causing the trouble, merely as a favor. Another time, after Ford had okayed a Worthington prototype for a Lincoln Continental part, Szuba and Armbruster were surprised when the parts cracked during assembly at the Ford plant. Upon testing the parts, Worthington discovered another company's steel had been used, and the supplier admitted to cutting costs by going with a different processing company.

"The vendor changed suppliers for a three-cent savings," said Szuba, "but when they failed, we had to pull Lincoln Continentals off the line until the Worthington guys arrived. It proved to us what we had with Worthington. The quality difference was like night and day."

The corporate relationship that began with a sales call has "benefited Ford tremendously," according to Joe Szuba, and benefited Worthington as well. Ford has remained a loyal customer of the steel processor. It comes as no surprise to Ted Armbruster, now the director of technical services at Worthington Industries. "It's the way we succeed," he said. "We strive to become the customer's metallurgist. We want to be the steel expert for each of our customers."

including power, cutting and welding tools; medical oxygen containers; fire extinguishers; and scuba gear.[65] Based in Austria, the company had sales of $40 million.[66]

The acquisition was praised by market analysts for adding to Worthington's core strengths. Robert Schenosky, an analyst with Merrill Lynch Global Securities of New York, noted that although Worthington had problems generating the kind of returns it wanted on its plastics and precision metals operations, "The cylinder business is one of the operations Worthington has excelled at.... We see this as a positive, as the company has been repositioning itself over the last year."[67]

The Heiser purchase was the first step of a European shopping spree for Worthington Cylinders. In February, Worthington purchased a majority interest in Gastec spol. a.r.o., the Czech Republic's leading pressure cylinder manufacturer.[68] Three months later, the cylinder group bought the assets of Metalurgica Progresso de Vale de Cambra, Lda.[69] Based near Porto, Portugal, Progresso's cylinder division produced small and medium-size LPG cylinders used in heating and industrial applications.

"These acquisitions are important elements of our global strategy to establish leadership positions in all segments of our business," said Winland. "They broaden our existing European manufacturing base and provide us with low-pressure cylinder products to complement our high-pressure capabilities at Joseph Heiser in Austria. Progresso positions us to serve the western European LPG markets, and Gastec gives us a base to serve the developing eastern European markets."[70]

By 1998, the division operated seven wholly owned facilities and offered the industry's most comprehensive line of products.[71] Almost 30 years after the original acquisition of its cylinder division, Worthington produced more than 13 million cylinders and shipped them to more than 50 countries.[72]

Divestiture: Finding Its Strengths

In the midst of these acquisitions, John P. McConnell began to pursue a different kind of strategy, one he had long believed in. On April 2,

business," he noted.[64] South America was a prime market in the late 1990s because home use of propane was widespread in rural areas, where electricity was expensive (if available at all) and natural gas pipelines were rare.

In June 1998, Worthington again expanded the cylinder division with the acquisition of Europe's leading producer of high pressure cylinders, Joseph Heiser vormals J. Winter's Sohn GmbH. Heiser manufactured cylinders for a variety of uses,

Above: In 1999, *Fortune* magazine released its first list of "The 100 Best Companies to Work for in America." Worthington Industries, with one of the lowest voluntary turnover rates, was a featured company.

Right: In 2001, after two years as head of Worthington Cylinders, Virgil Winland was promoted to senior vice president, manufacturing. During his tenure at Worthington Cylinders, the division rapidly moved overseas and began developing a new product for helium balloons.

1998, *The Wall Street Journal* reported that Worthington was "exploring" the sale of three units that made up more than a quarter of its total revenues.[73] These three were Worthington Custom Plastics, Worthington Precision Metals and Buckeye Steel Castings. Together they employed approximately 5,500 people at 13 locations and accounted for 26 percent of the company's 1997 revenues.[74]

Worthington's "long-term strategic plans," wrote Chris Adams in *The Wall Street Journal*, were to "focus more on core steel operations."[75] Sales at the steel unit had jumped 28 percent over the previous three-year period, compared to 26 percent for custom products and a drop for steel castings.[76] More than 80 percent of the $1 billion Worthington had poured into capital projects and acquisitions in the six years previous were related to steel.[77]

"Management's focus has clearly been on enhancing our leadership position in value-added steel processing and steel-related niche markets," John P. McConnell agreed.[78] *The Wall Street Journal* went on to discuss why divesting non-steel-related businesses was a good idea:

> *"Analysts said it could be in Worthington's best interests to sell the units — and in fact it might have made sense to sell them a few years ago. 'The competition in the plastics industry has been consolidating, and Worthington either has to get bigger in plastics or sell,' said Aldo Mazzaferro Jr., an analyst with Deutsche Morgan Grenfell, Inc. 'In order to maintain their role as a strong player in plastics, they would have to invest significant sums of money.'"*[79]

Led by a strong fourth quarter, 1998 was a solid year, with earnings up 24 percent and sales of more than $1.6 billion.[80] By the time the figures were released, the decision to move forward as a streamlined company had been made.

"We made an important strategic decision," said John P. McConnell, "to continue our focus on steel processing and metals-related businesses. These core competencies represent our strengths and offer the best opportunities to maximize shareholder value."[81]

The divestitures were completed in less than a year. In November, Worthington sold its Precision Metals subsidiary and Dietrich Industries' garage door division.[82] In February 1999, Buckeye Steel Castings was sold to Key Equity Capital Corporation, a Cleveland-based investment team.[83]

Joe Harden, Buckeye's president and CEO, said, "The good news for our employees and for Columbus is that Buckeye Steel will continue to operate as a strong company. We are proud of the nearly 20-year partnership with Worthington Industries and understand their decision to concentrate on their core operations."[84]

In April, Morton Industrial Group, a metal and plastic components manufacturer, obtained Worthington's $100 million nonautomotive Custom Plastics business, including facilities located in Lebanon, Kentucky; St. Matthews, South Carolina; and Harrisburg, North Carolina.[85] Six weeks later, Key Equity Capital Corporation purchased the automotive division of Worthington Custom Plastics, with $200 million in annual sales, 2,000 employees and three plants, in addition to a program management, engineering and design office in Troy, Michigan.[86]

A Time to Reorganize

Worthington emerged from the sales a leaner, more focused company. Still, there was room for improvement. In growing from a single plant to a sprawling corporation, Worthington had maintained its "country store" approach. Each facility had its own general manager, vice president of sales, and profit and loss statements. This structure had the disadvantage of generating internal competition and not allowing plants to use excess capabilities because work was not typically shifted between plants. As the processing industry grew more capital intensive and technically sophisticated, however, Worthington realized it could benefit from a more team-oriented approach.

In May 1999, the company announced a reorganization of its steel group into larger, regional strategic business units, or SBUs. These SBUs were designed to "better align our existing employees, plants and equipment to give us a more competitive

Above: The nation's largest specialty steel processor, Worthington's steel processing division accounted for 80 percent of the company's $1.5 billion in annual sales in 1999. The division had thousands of customers, including some of the world's largest manufacturing companies, and they produced everything from cars to home appliances.

Below: Ralph Roberts was named president of the Steel Group after Worthington reorganized the operation into a single division in 1999. Two years later, Roberts was promoted to senior vice president, marketing.

advantage in the marketplace," according to John P. McConnell.[87] Under the new structure, no general manager would run any individual plant. Rather, a team of operations managers was assigned to regions that included several plants. Sales teams were also no longer assigned to individual plants but were organized along product lines.[88]

The more centralized approach mirrored the highly successful structures at Dietrich and in the cylinder division. Ralph Roberts, who was named president of Worthington Steel, the largest operating group, explained some of the benefits in a message to employees:

"We can use our size to leverage our purchasing position. Operating as 'country stores,' our plants purchased their own steel based on customer orders. This meant we presented ourselves to the steel mills as a number of small- to mid-sized customers. As one steel company, we are one of the largest purchasers of steel in the

country. That means we can negotiate better prices and service with the mills....

"Second, we will be more efficient in how we deploy our plants and people. Working as regions rather than individual plants, we're in a better position to make sure we're using our assets to maximum potential and to eliminate redundancies in our system."[89]

Furthermore, Roberts noted, Worthington's customers would benefit. Under the old approach, "A big customer for Plant A might be a relatively small customer for Plant B, meaning that same customer might get much better price and service at one plant versus another.... That's not going to happen when we work as one steel company."[90]

At heart, the restructuring was all about teamwork — a familiar concept to the employees at Worthington. Whereas the former system had put general managers totally in charge of the process of their plants — the relationships, the profitability and the investment — the new structure emphasized a combined approach.

"The general manager won't be responsible for all those elements across the board," said Christie.

"He'll receive a tremendous amount of help. He'll have more of a team. But the operations of the individual plants on getting product in and getting product out and meeting customers, that responsibility is one of the highest responsibilities in Worthington Industries. The day-to-day functions may change. The responsibilities and the importance to this company won't change at all."[91]

On May 31, a day before the reorganization took effect, the changes at Worthington Industries were embodied in the retirement of Don Malenick after 41 years of service, 23 of them as president and chief operating officer. Malenick had begun his career in 1958 as a day laborer for the fledgling business and had helped guide the company's success.

"Don is a leader in the industry, and his knowledge of the business has helped the company position itself as the country's leading steel processor and

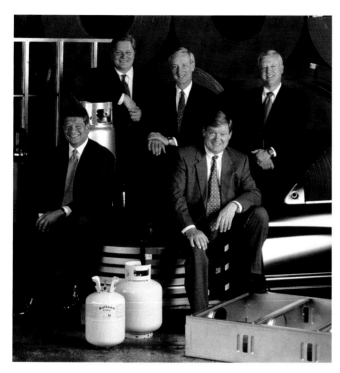

As part of a 2001 reorganization of the executive ranks, new leaders moved into operating positions while the company struggled with a depressed global market for steel. Clockwise from top left are Ed Ponko, president, Dietrich Metal Framing; Ed Ferkany, president, Worthington Steel; Ken Vagnini, president, Gerstenslager; John Christie, president and chief operating officer, Worthington Industries; and John Lamprinakos, president, Worthington Cylinders.

a leading manufacturer of metals-related products," said John P. McConnell.[92]

During Malenick's retirement party, a video was shown that General Counsel Dale Brinkman used as an example of the kind of managers Worthington has developed. Like John H. McConnell, Malenick had spent years walking through Worthington's plants, talking to workers and staying involved in the daily production. "On that video, a lot of the plant guys talked to Don like he was their old buddy," Brinkman said. "It was just like an old fishing buddy was retiring, and they had that relationship because he walked through the plant every day."[93]

An Industry Suffers

When it came to filling the empty positions of president and COO, Worthington turned to John Christie, president of JMAC. A former senior vice president of Ameritrust Bank, Christie held an MBA in finance and marketing from Emory University. John P. McConnell lauded Christie's reputation "for being a team builder."[94]

"Very few companies have the strong foundation that's been developed at Worthington," Christie remarked after his promotion. "When people read about a new leader, one of their biggest questions is 'Does this guy understand the basic philosophy on which this company was built?' I've worked with this philosophy my whole life. People are our biggest asset. In fact, at JMAC, we have put employee profit sharing into every small company we buy. We're trying to put the Worthington philosophy into every company."[95]

Although slimmer in the wake of its divestitures and reorganization, Worthington Industries was poised for growth — which posed another kind of challenge. In its first 50 years, the standard for Worthington's behavior was set by John H. McConnell. Sometimes called the "Worthington Way," this principle demanded that Worthington employees respect and honor the dignity of their coworkers, customers and vendors.

Yet maintaining this special culture of fairness, caring, hard work and compassion became harder as Worthington grew — and the concept was again tested in 2000 and into the first few years of the new millennium. Worthington had just had its principles tested when the Monroe plant burned, but no one could have expected that another major challenge would arise so soon. Just about the time that John Christie settled into his new office, the steel industry began a cyclical downturn. At the time, the U.S. economy was still strong, and the problems in steel were viewed as the continuing struggle of the integrated mills to survive and the effects of global oversupply.

By 2001, however, it was obvious that deeper forces were at work. With the manufacturing industry already mired in a recession, in March 2001, shortly after President George W. Bush was elected, the U.S. economy slipped into recession for the first time in a decade. This turnabout exacerbated the already weakened automotive, technology and steel industries.

Then, on September 11, 2001, terrorists attacked and destroyed the World Trade Center and part of the Pentagon and caused a hijacked plane to crash in rural Pennsylvania. The effects were immediate and devastating. Some 3,000 people were killed. For a week afterward, no airplanes flew in the United States. The stock markets were closed. Economic activity in the country ground to a halt.

"The first order of business was to make sure that everybody we had in the field was safe and able to put an anchor down while we waited to see how we could get them back," said Cathy Mayne Lyttle, vice president, communications. "Then, on that Friday, we had a moment of silence, and we shut down production in Columbus, gathered with J. P. outside and spent a few minutes in silence with the American flag."[96]

Worthington, fortunately, lost no employees in the terrorist attacks, but the already weakened economy reeled, and nowhere was the situation worse than in the automotive and steel industries. Automotive companies had been suffering, but after September 11, General Motors announced a zero-percent-interest financing deal to prevent a rout in the industry. Other manufacturers quickly followed suit. Car sales dropped — although not as much as they might have — and the automobile companies lost millions in finance interest. Naturally, the downturn in car sales affected any company in the steel industry, whether it was a supplier producing assemblies or a steel company rolling slabs. "Practically all of our customers, excluding General Motors, are losing money," remarked Ken Vagnini in early 2002.[97]

Already faced with cheap imports, falling demand and too much inventory, and burdened by huge pension plans, the giant integrated steel manufacturers began to hemorrhage money. By June 2001, 18 U.S. steel manufacturers had already filed for bankruptcy protection. After September 11, the bankruptcies continued. By late 2001, bankrupt steel manufacturers included LTV, the nation's third-largest steel producer, and Trico.[98] Although most of these bankruptcies didn't affect Worthington directly, the sudden demise of Trico struck close to home, remembered Ed Ferkany.

"They went straight into Chapter 7, and it posed a very serious problem for us," Ferkany said. "They were a major supplier to us, and we had to replace them and not miss any orders at the same time. Fortunately, other mills, particularly U.S. Steel and Bethlehem, stepped up and supported us."[99]

To relieve the foundering steel industry, steelmakers petitioned the Bush administration for federal trade protection and government assumption of the costly pension plans. Critics of the plan argued that integrated mills had brought these troubles on themselves by failing to innovate with new manufacturing technologies. For proof, they pointed to the minimills, such as Nucor and Steel Dynamics, which continued to post record profits. Despite the rancorous debate, the Bush administration went ahead with tariffs in early 2002, instituting the most sweeping tariffs on imports since the Hawley-Smoot tariffs of 1930.

Throughout these remarkable challenges to its industry, Worthington showed leadership, both internally and externally. In January 2001, CEO John P. McConnell announced several changes in the executive ranks. Mark Stier announced his retirement, and another Worthington veteran, Harry Goussetis, was named vice president, human resources. At the same time, Ralph Roberts, president of Worthington Steel, was named senior vice president of marketing for Worthington Industries, and Ed Ferkany was brought back to run Worthington Steel. Ferkany had run the division from 1985 to 1998 and was only months from retirement when he was tapped for the new position.

"When I came back, we were in the midst of correcting our inventory position," Ferkany said. "We were overinventoried due to rapid change in the marketplace."[100]

In Worthingon Cylinders, Virgil Winland was named senior vice president of manufacturing for Worthington Industries, manufacturing, and John Lamprinakos, a 22-year veteran with Worthington, was named president. Similar to his counterpart in steel, Lamprinakos inherited a fragile business. "A good piece of our business is geared toward barbecue gas grills," he said in late 2001. "With the economy hurting, people do not have the income to spend in the backyard."[101]

Moreover, after years of effort overseas, the cylinder business was hurt by the weakened global economy, especially in South America, where Argentina was suffering a financial meltdown and Brazil's economy was shaky. Hoping to increase sales, Worthington Cylinders was planning to expand its product line with the Balloon Time™ cylinder, a helium tank to fill balloons.

Worthington Responds

As the new leadership took position, John P. McConnell explained to the press why it was necessary to invigorate the divisions. "All of these changes are vital and important to our company strategy," he said. "The new corporate officers will be instrumental in developing new leaders and succession plans.... As we work through a challenging time for the steel industry, these changes are critical to prepare us for our goal of future growth."[102]

Even with these changes, sales would recover only slowly while the general economy continued to limp along. In May 2001, Worthington announced that sales had slipped that year, down nearly 7 percent to $1.827 billion.[103]

"Although fourth quarter earnings were the best of the year, nothing will change the fact that fiscal 2001 was one of the most challenging in the company's history," John P. McConnell announced. "The difficulties of the U.S. manufacturing sector, especially the steel industry, are well publicized, and Worthington has not been immune."[104]

Ultimately, Worthington would take until well into 2002 to begin its turnaround, swimming upstream against a recessive economy and buffeted by a wild steel industry. The Bush tarriffs and the sudden removal of huge steel producers through bankruptcy combined to produce a sudden shortage in supply. Prices of steel in the United States skyrocketed throughout 2002, and Worthington, as a fabricator, was stuck in the middle.

Nevertheless, the company had a plan and was determined to stick with it: Inventory would be tightened, some prices would be raised, and the workforce be reduced through attrition and layoffs. This effort produced strong earnings for 2001/2002 even as sales continued to slide. By December 2001, Worthington stock was "near a 52-week high," reported *The Columbus Dispatch*. "Analysts said Worthington Industries is seeing earnings rise

because it has cut costs, spent capital judiciously, and improved inventory management."[105]

By 2002 the economic outlook had begun to brighten, and Worthington continued to take the necessary steps. In January, John P. McConnell announced that Worthington would embark on a comprehensive consolidation plan. The company would take a $65 million charge against earnings in conjunction with the plan, which would shutter six plants and reduce the employee count at two other facilities over the next 12 months. A metal framing plant in Virginia was closed, and its work was transferred to the plant in Rock Hill, South Carolina, which would service both processed steel and metal framing customers. Worthington Cylinders discontinued operations in Claremore, Oklahoma, and withdrew from its partnerships in Brazil. In processed steel, plants were closed at Malvern, Pennsylvania, and Jackson, Michigan, and overhead was reduced at Louisville, Kentucky.

In typical Worthington fashion, every effort was made to help the employees who were affected by the consolidation plan. Overall, about 500 employees were laid off as Worthington reduced its worldwide workforce by 7 percent.

"Today's action delivers on a commitment that we made to our shareholders to ensure that our business segments are maximizing profitability," McConnell told *The Columbus Dispatch*.[106] At the same time, analysts were caught a little by surprise. Worthington had improved its earnings near the end of 2001, and the consolidation was widely seen as a way for the company to restore competitiveness in a down market.

The Upside

Worthington's response to the trying times was typical of the company. It was reasoned, compassionate, and intelligent. Once again, the company's leadership was recognized and rewarded. Less than two weeks after announcing the most comprehensive reorganization in its history, Worthington Industries was named to *Fortune* magazine's list of "100 Best Companies to Work For."[107] In the next month's issue, *Fortune* declared that Worthington was one of "America's Most Admired Companies."[108] Later in the year, on the basis of the company's excellent historical rate of return and its rising stock price, *Money* magazine picked Worthington as one its 30 best-performing stocks over the last 30 years.[109]

This praise was not due only to Worthington's aggressive streamlining. Rather, even through the worst of the downturn and the highest steel prices, the company had continued to look for innovative ways to approach its market and profit. A new product, a steel pallet called Steelpac, was just one example of this drive for profitability. The idea for a steel pallet actually came from a Worthington steel customer, remembered Worthington Vice President Pat Cotter, who was in charge of the project.

"It was started at the request of Harley-Davidson," Cotter said.

"Harley-Davidson came to us and said they had an issue with the wood pallets. So we went into research and development on plastic pallets and steel pallets, and after a year, both companies concurred that the steel pallet was the best way to solve Harley's problem."[110]

During its market research, Worthington discovered a huge potential market for steel pallets. In fact, the market was estimated at $4.5 billion annually, and the steel pallet boasted several advantages over wood. Not only was it much stronger, but the steel pallet was also more environmentally friendly because it could be recycled. "There is no waste," Cotter said. "It just goes to a scrap dealer who puts it back into the mill, melts it down, and makes a car out of it. We're getting multiple returns on our pallets."[111]

Steelpac's final advantage accrued to Worthington itself. In a down market, the Steelpac Group offered Worthington a chance to benefit from potential vertical integration. In the future,

---

The Steelpac recyclable steel pallet was originally designed for customer Harley-Davidson. Sensing an opportunity, Worthington Steelpac began to aggressively promote the innovative pallets to a variety of industries.

much of the steel for the pallets would be purchased from Gerstenslager, which had recently opened a new plant in Clyde, Ohio. "We have a great relationship with Steelpac," Vagnini said. "We are looking at ways to stamp and assemble parts that are nonautomotive in nature."[112]

TradeReady®

Dietrich, Worthington's framing business, developed the most visible example of Worthington's will to succeed: the TradeReady framing system. This innovative system substituted steel for the traditional wooden components of housing construction, such as floor joists.

Steel had powerful advantages in residential and light commercial construction. First and foremost, of course, were strength and durability. A floor built on steel floor joists would never warp or succumb to moisture or termites and could withstand great environmental pressures, such as hurricanes. Furthermore, TradeReady framing units already had holes punched through them so other contractors — electrical, plumbing, heating and telecommunications — could easily run wiring under the floors or behind walls.

Almost immediately after announcing TradeReady, Dietrich followed up with an agreement with Centex, one of the largest residential home builders in the United States, to use TradeReady products in its homes. This relationship, of course, required that Worthington conduct a major educational campaign to teach housing contractors how to install the innovative steel frames.

"I'm very fond of saying that while the Greeks invented concrete, Romans perfected it, and Christ was a carpenter," said Ed Ponko, president of Dietrich.

"There's two millennia of framing materials that people are familiar with. Metal framing history is not nearly as long, so it's just a lot of retraining. We have TradeReady specialists equipped with laptops who can identify problems and check with another TradeReady rep. They're equipped with trucks and all the appropriate tools and actually go to job sites and instruct people familiar with wood how to use steel."[113]

With its early successes, Dietrich was ready to expand TradeReady and in summer 2002 announced a large, strategic acquisition. Worthington had negotiated the purchase of Unimast Incorporated, the second-largest producer of steel framing products, behind only Dietrich itself. This acquisition, valued at about $120 million, was the second-largest acquisition in Worthington's history, surpassed only by Dietrich. It was a perfect strategic fit. When *Money* magazine picked Worthington stock as a winner, the magazine commented, "This company has thrived by moving into housing and other new areas outside its core auto market."[114]

According to Ponko, the Unimast acquisition rounded out Dietrich's metal framing product line, and senior management generally agreed that it provided major growth opportunities for Worthington.

"Unimast was principally located in the eastern two thirds of the United States," Ponko said.

"There were synergies in that a lot of their revenue and profits were generated by products that we didn't have, but that augmented what we did have. We picked up a vinyl trim business, a metal lath business, and a Clinchon metal corner bead, which has high brand visibility. And obviously, Unimast had a significant position in the design community for metal framing."[115]

Overall, Unimast brought 800 employees and a number of new facilities to Worthington. During the last half of 2002, the companies worked to merge and consolidate their operations. "We've been going in on a weekly basis and coverting one Unimast facility to our information system," Ponko said. "And we have ten facilities to intergrate, as well as integrating the employees to our health care and our benefit systems, and more importantly, to our incentive pay systems."[116]

Shortly after Unimast, Worthington made another strategic acquisition, a company called Enertech. Valued at only around $2 million, Enertech was nevertheless an important acquisition because of its unique construction management business. Worthington was able to offer a turnkey solution to builders of residential and light commercial construction projects.

"Enertech is there to get us a little bit more attuned to the applicators' world," Ponko said. "We will be able to go out and convert anything that is not already specified in metal framing. While we're doing that, we have a couple of unique systems in terms of using our floor and bypass framing. We'll be getting some hands-on experience where we can actually go out and either manage construction projects to use metal framing or actually do some of them ourselves. Our long-term goal is to manage the construction projects, meaning we would look at facilities that specified wood and masonry and we would offer a turnkey solution, put the bid in, and contract it out to our core subcontractors."[117]

Within Worthington, there was a palpable sense of excitement surrounding this new project, one that extended throughout senior management.

Dietrich's TradeReady steel framing system comes predrilled with holes for electricity, plumbing, air conditioning and other necessities. It is more convenient and stronger than wood framing.

"We are meeting with great success," said company President John Christie. "From a marketing expansion, we've really taken an aggressive approach in the residential side of metal framing."[118]

Sticking to the Path

Through its new products and reorganization, Worthington Industries continued to outperform the steel industry and regain strong profitability. "We had some assets that were dragging us down," Christie said.

"We made a conscious decision to exit from some areas of business, and our other assets have been much more highly productive because of the movement of customers into more efficient facilities. Plus, we've made strategic acquisitions. We are very poised for growth when the economy picks up."[119]

This position came in large part from the depth of Worthington's executive suite: The company's officers have hundreds of years of combined experience. As it grew and needed different

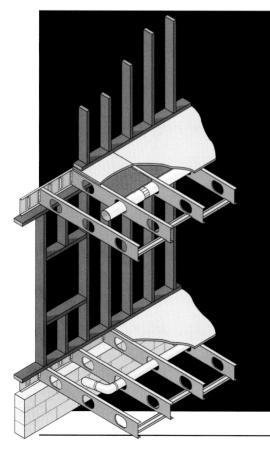

Benefits of The Dietrich TradeReady® Floor System

- No squeaky floors

- More predictable material costs

- Fire, termite and corrosion resistant

- Greatly reduced waste

- Compatible with wood, masonry and light gauge metal framing

- Capable of supporting longer spans to help reduce material costs

- No need to cut holes for HVAC, plumbing and electrical

- Stronger, lighter, more consistently straight than wood

sorts of expertise, Worthington also began to bring in executives at high levels of management. John Baldwin was one of those executives. After a successful career as assistant treasurer at the giant Tenneco, he was hired into Worthington in 1997 as treasurer. Eight months later, he was promoted to CFO. The hiring process, Baldwin remembered, was long and demanding.

"When so much of the company is built on culture, there has to be a fit, and it's very difficult to determine if there's a cultural fit if you just have one interview. I think I must have visited here five times before an offer was forthcoming. Then, when I came here, I guess I was a little skeptical because you tend to think a company like Worthington doesn't hire too many people from the outside. You think it's going to be difficult to break in. But that couldn't have been further from the truth. People were very welcoming. They would thank me for working so hard or bringing a fresh perspective. People would actually thank me for my contribution. I was floored."[120]

At the same time, other people moved into powerful leadership positions. In 2002, Worthington announced that Ed Ferkany would return to retirement in early 2003. He had served his last stint as president of Worthington Steel during its reorganization, putting off his retirement by two years. As he left, John P. McConnell announced that Joe Harden would be the next president of Worthington Steel. At the time, Harden was president of Buckeye Steel Castings, where he had worked since 1973.

"As a former member of our senior leadership team, he is familiar with our unique history, culture and philosophy, and is well known and trusted in the organization," said John P. McConnell.[121]

A Leader Steps Away

The need for cultural leadership was even more pressing as the company grew and evolved. By 2002, Worthington Industries was a $2 billion company with 62 facilities in 10 countries and more than 8,000 employees. Throughout its history, Worthington had consistently posted strong financial returns while maintaining some of the best employee relationships of any manufacturing company in the United States. Of all its plants only a minority were unionized, and those plants had come with acquisitions. A number of the facilities decertified the union after becoming part of Worthington. Founded on deep-rooted principles, Worthington had proven that good business and good ethics go hand in hand, and the company maintained relationships with charities and organizations including YMCA, the United Way, Children's Hospital, Junior Achievement, and Goodwill.

"It's been instilled in everybody at Worthington that it's important to give back, whether you do it in small, quiet ways in your child's PTA or even bigger ways," said Cathy Mayne Lyttle.[122]

Although it took thousands of people to build this legacy, none deserved so much credit as John H. McConnell, the company's founder and first leader. In 2002, more than 47 years after launching the company, John H. took his final steps away from Worthington Industries. At that year's shareholder's meeting, 79-year-old John H. announced he was retiring from Worthinton's board of directors. He had retired as CEO in 1993 and as chairman in 1996. When asked by *The Columbus Dispatch* what he planned to do, McConnell said he would "sit back, enjoy life and not worry about a thing."[123]

John H. McConnell would never truly be absent from Worthington Industries, however. During the shareholder's meeting, John P. showed an emotional crowd a moving video tribute of his father's lifework.

"Stepping down as CEO was really the big move," the younger McConnell later said. "And it's not like he's going anywhere, but for some reason, it was a very, very emotional event."[124]

Heading into the future, buoyed by a rising stock price, new directions and products, new leadership and an age-old Golden Rule, Worthington is as well positioned as any company in its industry. It has collected national awards and recognition through even the roughest waters of the 2001 recession, and it has managed to steer a steady course while the steel industry has fluctuated wildly.

"We're trying to align ourselves with the steel supply base in the United States, and we've outperformed the market by 200 percent," said John P. McConnell in late 2002. "We've had a nice run over the last year."[125]

Notes to Sources

Chapter One

1. John H. McConnell, *And We've Only Scratched the Surface: The Growth Story of Worthington Industries* (New York: The Newcomen Society of North America, 1981), p. 5.
2. John H. McConnell, interviewed by the author, October 23, 1998. Transcript, p. 1.
3. Ibid., pp. 3-4.
4. Ibid.
5. John Hoerr, *And the Wolf Finally Came: The Decline of the American Steel Industry* (Pittsburgh: University of Pittsburgh Press, 1988), p. 164.
6. Ibid.
7. Ibid.
8. Ibid.
9. Ibid., p. 86.
10. Ibid.
11. Ibid., p. 165.
12. Ibid., p. 88.
13. Ibid., p. 86.
14. Ibid., p. 89.
15. Ibid., p. 164.
16. Ibid.
17. John H. McConnell, interviewed by the author, October 23, 1998. Transcript, p. 8.
18. Ibid., p. 9.
19. John H. McConnell, "A Message for the Future," *The Open Door* (summer 1988), p. 1.
20. Ibid.
21. John H. McConnell, interviewed by the author, October 23, 1998. Transcript, p. 6.
22. Ibid.
23. John H. McConnell, "A Message for the Future," *The Open Door* (summer 1988), p. 1.
24. Ibid.
25. John H. McConnell, interviewed by the author, October 23, 1998. Transcript, p. 10.
26. H.G. Cordero and L.H. Tarring. *Babylon to Birmingham* (London: Quin Press Ltd.), p. 268.
27. Hoerr, p. 96.
28. Christopher Hall, *Steel Phoenix: The Fall and Rise of the U.S. Steel Industry* (New York: St. Martin's, 1997), p. 4.
29. Hoerr, p. 464.
30. John H. McConnell, interviewed by the author, October 23, 1998. Transcript, p. 12.
31. Ibid., p. 14.
32. Ibid.
33. Ibid., p. 16.
34. Ibid.
35. Ibid., p. 18.
36. Ibid., pp. 17-18.
37. Ibid., p. 23.
38. Donald F. Barnett and Louis Schorsch, *Steel: Upheaval in a Basic Industry* (Cambridge, Massachusetts: Ballinger Publishing Company, 1983), p. 9.
39. Barnett and Schorsch, p. 22.
40. Hall, p. 35.
41. Ibid., p. 36.
42. Ibid.
43. Barnett and Schorsch, pp. 13-14.
44. John H. McConnell, interviewed by the author, October 23, 1998. Transcript, p. 25.
45. Ibid., p. 23.
46. Ibid., p. 24.
47. Hall, p. xiii.
48. John H. McConnell, *And We've Only Scratched the Surface: The Growth Story of Worthington Industries* (New York: The Newcomen Society of North America, 1981), pp. 8-9.

49. John H. McConnell, interviewed by the author, October 23, 1998. Transcript, pp. 29-30.

50. Ibid., p. 30.

51. Ibid.

Chapter One Sidebar: Behind the Walls

1. William Hogan, *Global Steel in the 1990s: Growth or Decline* (Lexington, Massachusetts: Lexington Books, 1991), p. 1.

2. Donald F. Barnett and Louis Schorsch, *Steel: Upheaval in a Basic Industry* (Cambridge, Massachusetts: Ballinger Publishing Company, 1983), p. 22.

3. Ibid.

4. Ibid., p. 23.

5. Christopher Hall, *Steel Phoenix: The Fall and Rise of the U.S. Steel Industry* (New York: St. Martin's, 1997), p. 37.

6. Ibid.

7. Barnett and Schorsch, pp. 25-26.

8. Donald Barnett and Ronald Crandall, *Up from the Ashes: The Rise of the Steel Minimill in the United States* (Washington, D.C.: The Brookings Institution, 1986), p. 3.

9. Barnett and Schorsch, p. 14.

10. Ibid., p. 28.

11. Ibid.

12. John Hoerr, *And the Wolf Finally Came: The Decline of the American Steel Industry* (Pittsburgh: University of Pittsburgh Press, 1988), p. 101.

13. Barnett and Schorsch, p. 32.

14. Hall, p. 44.

15. Barnett and Schorsch, p. 22.

Chapter Two

1. Worthington Industries 1995 Annual Report, p. 2.

2. John H. McConnell, interviewed by the author, October 23, 1998. Transcript, p. 31.

3. John H. McConnell, *And We've Only Scratched the Surface: The Growth Story of Worthington Industries* (New York: The Newcomen Society of North America, 1981), p. 5.

4. John H. McConnell, interviewed by the author, October 23, 1998. Transcript, p. 32.

5. Ibid.

6. "Margaret Orth Retires," *MetalPhonics* (October 1970), p. 7.

7. "The First Lady of Worthington Steel," *MetalPhonics* (July 1967), p. 6.

8. John H. McConnell, interviewed by the author, October 23, 1998. Transcript. p. 33.

9. Ibid.

10. Ibid.

11. Ibid.

12. Ibid.

13. Ibid., p. 34.

14. John H. McConnell, *And We've Only Scratched the Surface: The Growth Story of Worthington Industries* (New York: The Newcomen Society of North America, 1981), p. 10.

15. Internal records from Worthington Industries' Department of Investor Relations, office of Todd Rollins. Obtained from Doris Bogner, March 1999.

16. Ibid.

17. Ed Pati, interviewed by the author, April 14, 1999. Transcript, pp. 1, 6.

18. Ibid., p. 7.

19. Dick Whitehead, interviewed by the author, April 14, 1999. Transcript, p. 3.

20. John H. McConnell, interviewed by the author, October 23, 1998. Transcript, p. 32.

21. Chris Jones, interviewed by Lisa Allen. Date unknown.

22. Ibid.

23. John H. McConnell, interviewed by the author, October 23, 1998. Transcript, pp. 34-35.

24. Ed Pati, interviewed by the author, April 14, 1999. Transcript, pp. 2-3.

25. Dick Whitehead, interviewed by the author, April 14, 1999. Transcript, p. 4.

26. Ibid., p. 14.

27. Internal records from Worthington Industries' Department of Investor Relations, office of Todd Rollins. Obtained from Doris Bogner, March 1999.

28. "Profile: De Johaning" *MetalPhonics* (June 1970), p. 4.

29. John H. McConnell, "Comments," *MetalPhonics* (February 1969), p. 1.

30. Ibid.

31. Christopher Hall, *Steel Phoenix: The Fall and Rise of the U.S. Steel Industry* (New York: St. Martin's, 1997), pp. 43, 46.

32. Ibid., p. 43.

33. Dick Whitehead, interviewed by the author, April 14, 1999. Transcript, p. 9.

34. Ibid., p. 2.

35. Ibid., p. 3.

36. Ibid.

37. "For Non-Ferrous, It's Scioto Metals," *MetalPhonics* (February-March 1965), p. 1.

38. Ibid.

39. Donald F. Barnett and Louis Schorsch, *Steel: Upheaval in a Basic Industry* (Cambridge, Massachusetts: Ballinger Publishing Company, 1983), p. 42.

40. Hall, p. 260.

41. Tom Peters, "Role Model in Steel," *U.S. News & World Report* (January 20, 1986).

42. Hall, p. 60.
43. Ibid.
44. Ibid., p. 156.
45. Ibid., p. 60.
46. Barnett and Schorsch, p. 85.
47. Ibid., p. 88.
48. John H. McConnell, interviewed by the author, October 23, 1998. Transcript, p. 36.
49. Ibid., p. 37.
50. Jeff Phillips, "The Son Also Rises," *Columbus CEO* (April 1995), p. 1.
51. John H. McConnell, "Comments," *MetalPhonics* (February 1969), p. 1.
52. Ibid.
53. "Worthington Steel's Louisville, Ky. Operations Serve Six States," *MetalPhonics* (September-October 1964), pp. 1-3.
54. Ibid.
55. Internal records from Worthington Industries' Department of Investor Relations, office of Todd Rollins. Obtained from Doris Bogner, March 1999.
56. Ralph Roberts, interviewed by the author, October 23, 1998. Transcript, p. 6.
57. Rob Swords, Jeff Glastettr, and Mary Wood-Andersen, interviewed by Lisa Allen. Date unknown.
58. Barnett and Schorsch, pp. 296-297.
59. Merwin Ray, "Steel Sales Scope," *MetalPhonics* (November-December 1963), p. 2.
60. Ibid.
61. Worthington Industries 1995 Annual Report, p. 7.
62. John H. McConnell, interviewed by the author, October 23, 1998. Transcript, p. 26.
63. Ibid.
64. Merwin Ray, "Steel Sales Scope," *MetalPhonics* (November-December 1963), p. 2

65. John H. McConnell, interviewed by the author, October 23, 1998. Transcript, p. 27.
66. Internal records from Worthington Industries' Department of Investor Relations, office of Todd Rollins. Obtained from Doris Bogner, March 1999.
67. John H. McConnell, "Comments," *MetalPhonics* (February 1969), p. 1.
68. Doc Burnquist, interviewed by David Patten, September 20, 1999. Transcript, p. 8.
69. "AccuTolerance Assures Uniform Thickness," *MetalPhonics* (November-December 1963), pp. 1, 4.
70. Merwin Ray, "Steel Sales Scope," *MetalPhonics* (November-December 1963), p. 2.
71. "Louisville Service Center," *MetalPhonics* (September-October 1964), p. 2.
72. Ray, p. 2.
73. "Louisville Service Center," *MetalPhonics* (September-October 1964), p. 3.
74. "Worthington Steel's Louisville, Ky. Operations Serve Six States," *MetalPhonics* (September-October 1964), p. 1.
75. Ibid.
76. Internal records from Worthington Industries' Department of Investor Relations, office of Todd Rollins. Obtained from Doris Bogner, March 1999.
77. Ray, p. 2.
78. Internal records from Worthington Industries' Department of Investor Relations, office of Todd Rollins. Obtained from Doris Bogner, March 1999.
79. "10th Anniversary Marks Expansion for Worthington Steel," *MetalPhonics* (August-September 1965), p. 1.
80. John H. McConnell, "Comments," *MetalPhonics*

(August-September 1965), p. 1.
81. "New Facilities Completed," *MetalPhonics* (December 1966), p. 1.
82. Ibid.
83. "Malenick Named VP-Manufacturing," *MetalPhonics* (July 1967), p. 2.
84. Internal records from Worthington Industries' Department of Investor Relations, office of Todd Rollins. Obtained from Doris Bogner, March 1999.
85. "Steel Buyers Attend WSC Seminar Sessions," *MetalPhonics* (July 1967), p. 1.
86. Merwin Ray, "Steel Sales Scope," *MetalPhonics* (July 1967), p. 2.
87. Erik Battenberg, "McConnell's Story is American Dream," *The Booster* (September 15, 1993), p. 22.
88. Ed Pati, interviewed by the author, April 14, 1998. Transcript, p. 11.
89. Jeff Phillips, "The Son Also Rises," *Columbus CEO* (April 1995), p. 1. Reprint.
90. John H. McConnell, *And We've Only Scratched the Surface: The Growth Story of Worthington Industries* (New York: The Newcomen Society in North America, 1980), p. 11.
91. Ibid.
92. Tom Peters, "Role Model in Steel," *U.S. News & World Report* (January 20, 1986).
93. Howard Rudnitsky, "You have to Trust the Workforce," *Forbes* (July 19, 1993), p. 78.
94. Don Malenick, interviewed by the author, October 23, 1998. Transcript, p. 19.
95. Harold "Red" Poling, interviewed by the author, September 28, 1999. Transcript, p. 4.

96. Tom Peters and Nancy Austin, *A Passion for Excellence: The Leadership Difference* (New York: Random House, 1985), p. 313.
97. Ibid.
98. John P. McConnell, interviewed by the author, October 23, 1998. Transcript, p. 4.
99. Ron Carter, "Man of Steel," *The Columbus Dispatch* (September 29, 1996), p. 1A.
100. Erik Battenberg, "McConnell's Story is American Dream," *The Booster* (September 15, 1993), p. 22.
101. Ibid.
102. Robert Levering and Milton Moskowitz, *The 100 Best Companies to Work for in America* (New York: Doubleday, 1993), p. 492.
103. John H. McConnell, *And We've Only Scratched the Surface: The Growth Story of Worthington Industries* (New York: The Newcomen Society in North America, 1980), p. 15.
104. Ibid.
105. Levering and Moskowitz, p. 491.
106. John H. McConnell, *And We've Only Scratched the Surface: The Growth Story of Worthington Industries* (New York: The Newcomen Society in North America, 1980), p. 16.
107. John P. McConnell, interviewed by the author, October 23, 1998. Transcript, p. 8.
108. John H. McConnell, *And We've Only Scratched the Surface: The Growth Story of Worthington Industries* (New York: The Newcomen Society in North America, 1980), p. 12.
109. Ron Carter, "Man of Steel," *The Columbus Dispatch* (September 29, 1996), p. 1F.

110. Kenny Shane, interviewed by David Patten, October 13, 1999. Transcript, p. 2.
111. John P. McConnell, interviewed by the author, October 23, 1998. Transcript, p. 8.
112. John H. McConnell, *And We've Only Scratched the Surface: The Growth Story of Worthington Industries* (New York: The Newcomen Society in North America, 1980), p. 12.
113. Ibid.
114. Ibid.
115. Ibid.
116. Ibid.
117. "Worthington Steel Establishes Ultra-Modern Employee Policies," *MetalPhonics* (June-July 1966), p. 1.
118. Ibid., pp. 1,2.
119. "1968 Good Profit Sharing Year," *MetalPhonics* (February 1969), p. 4.
120. Levering and Moskowitz, p. 490.
121. John H. McConnell, *And We've Only Scratched the Surface: The Growth Story of Worthington Industries* (New York: The Newcomen Society in North America, 1980), p. 12.
122. Ibid., p. 17.
123. Howard Rudnitsky, "You Have to Trust the Workforce," *Forbes* (July 19, 1993), p. 79.
124. Ibid.
125. Ibid.
126. Ron Carter, "Man of Steel," *The Columbus Dispatch* (September 29, 1996), p. 1F.
127. Rudnitsky, p. 79.
128. Ibid.
129. John H. McConnell, *And We've Only Scratched the Surface: The Growth Story of Worthington Industries* (New York: The Newcomen Society in North America, 1980), p. 17.

Chapter Two Sidebar: Employee Council

1. Robert Levering and Milton Moskowitz, *The 100 Best Companies to Work for in America* (New York: Currency Doubleday, 1993), p. 490.
2. John H. McConnell, *And We've Only Scratched the Surface: The Growth Story of Worthington Industries* (New York: The Newcomen Society in North America, 1981), p. 14.
3. Levering and Moskowitz, p. 490.

Chapter Two Sidebar: Malenick

1. Jeff Phillips, "The Son Also Rises," *Columbus CEO*, April 1995, p. 1 (Reprint).
2. Don Malenick, interviewed by the author, October 23, 1998. Transcript, p. 1.
3. Ibid., p. 2.
4. Ibid.
5. Ibid.
6. Ibid., p. 4.
7. Ibid.
8. Ibid., p. 5.

Chapter Three

1. Ralph Roberts, interviewed by the author, October 23, 1998. Transcript, p. 15.
2. The Worthington Steel Company 1969 Annual Report, p. 2.
3. Donald F. Barnett and Robert W. Crandall, *Up from the Ashes: The Rise of the Steel Minimill in the United States* (Washington: The Brookings Institution, 1986), p. 105.
4. Ibid.
5. The Worthington Steel Company 1969 Annual Report, p. 2.
6. "Worthington Steel Goes Public," *MetalPhonics* (February 1969), p. 2.
7. Ibid.

8. John H. McConnell, *And We've Only Scratched the Surface: The Growth Story of Worthington Industries* (New York: The Newcomen Society in North America, 1981), p. 17.

9. Worthington Steel 1969 Annual Report. p. 2.

10. Ibid.

11. John H. McConnell, "Comments," *MetalPhonics* (July 1969), p. 1.

12. Ibid.

13. The Worthington Steel Company 1969 Annual Report, p. 4.

14. Ibid.

15. Ibid.

16. Ibid.

17. Ibid.

18. Ibid.

19. Merwin Ray, "Industry Insight," *MetalPhonics* (February 1969), p. 2.

20. "Computers Take Over Paper Work, Speed Customer Service Calls," *Sales Management* (February 17, 1975), p. 18.

21. Worthington Steel 1969 Annual Report, p. 9.

22. "Computers Take Over Paper Work, Speed Customer Service Calls," *Sales Management* (February 17, 1975), p. 20.

23. Ibid.

24. "Armstrong Elected President of Worthington Industries," *MetalPhonics* (February 1974), p. 1.

25. "Worthington Steel's Testing Laboratory Provides New Service for Customers," *MetalPhonics* (November-December 1967), p. 1.

26. Ibid.

27. Ibid.

28. Ibid.

29. Merwin Ray, "Steel Sales Scope," *MetalPhonics* (November-December 1967), p. 2.

30. "Worthington Steel's Testing Laboratory Provides New Service for Customers," *MetalPhonics* (November-December 1967), p. 1.

31. Ibid.

32. "Corporate Stars that Brightened a Dark Decade," *Fortune* (April 30, 1984), p. 227.

33. The Worthington Steel Company 1970 Annual Report, p. 6.

34. The Worthington Steel Company 1971 Annual Report, p. 6.

35. The Worthington Steel Company 1970 Annual Report, p. 2.

36. Jack Graf, interviewed by David Patten, September 15, 1999. Transcript, p. 2.

37. Ike Kelley, interviewed by the author, April 14, 1999. Transcript, p. 18.

38. Merwin Ray, "Industry Insight," *MetalPhonics* (February 1969), p. 2.

39. "Inside Sales," *MetalPhonics* (October 1970), p. 4.

40. The Worthington Steel Company 1970 Annual Report, p. 3.

41. "Worthington Steel Marks Fifteenth Anniversary," *MetalPhonics* (October 1970), p. 1.

42. "Finance-Accounting Reorganized," *MetalPhonics* (January 1970), p. 1.

43. "Armstrong-McLaughlin Named Vice Presidents for Worthington Steel," *MetalPhonics* (June 1970), p. 2,

44. "Armstrong Elected President of Worthington Industries," *MetalPhonics* (February 1974), p. 1.

45. *MetalPhonics* (October 1970), pp. 5-6.

46. John H. McConnell, interviewed by the author, October 23, 1998. Transcript, p. 51.

47. "Introducing: Lennox Industries, Inc.," *MetalPhonics* (October 1970), p. 3.

48. Worthington Industries, Inc., 1972 Annual Report, p. 2.

49. Virgil Winland, interviewed by the author, April 15, 1999. Transcript, p. 3.

50. "Worthington Steel Forms Special Products Division," *MetalPhonics* (June 1971), p. 1.

51. Ibid., p. 2.

52. Worthington Industries, Inc., 1991 Annual Report, p. 4.

53. "Worthington Steel Forms Special Products Division," *MetalPhonics* (June 1971), p. 1.

54. The Worthington Steel Company 1971 Annual Report, p. 4.

**Chapter Three Sidebar:
Cylinder Manufacture...
The Perfect Fit**

1. Worthington Industries, Inc., 1991 Annual Report, p. 3.

2. Ibid., p. 5.

**Chapter Three Sidebar:
In Search of Rubber
SofteningCream**

1. Ike Kelley, interviewed by the author, April 14, 1999. Transcript, pp. 19-20.

2. Ibid.

3. Ralph Roberts, interviewed by the author, October 23, 1998. Transcript, p. 15.

Chapter Four

1. Ed Ferkany, interviewed by the author, April 14, 1998. Transcript, p. 8.

2. Christopher Hall, *Steel Phoenix: The Fall and Rise of the U.S. Steel Industry* (New York: St. Martins' Press, 1997), p. 61.

3. William T. Hogan, *Global Steel in the 1990s: Growth or Decline* (Lexington, MA: Lexington Books, 1991), p. 5.

4. Worthington Industries, Inc. 1972 Annual Report, p. 2.
5. Ibid., p. 1.
6. "Cylinder Division Plant Completed," *MetalPhonics* (October 1971), p. 1.
7. "Profit Sharing Hits New High," *MetalPhonics* (February 1971), p. 2.
8. The Worthington Steel Company 1971 Annual Report, p. 4.
9. John H. McConnell, *And We've Only Scratched the Surface: The Growth Story of Worthington Industries* (New York: The Newcomen Society in North America, 1981), pp. 14-15.
10. Ibid.
11. Ibid.
12. "CE Roundtable: Linking Employee and Enterprise Performance," *Chief Executive* (June 1994), p. 6.
13. Ralph Roberts, interviewed by the author, October 23, 1998. Transcript, pp. 3-4.
14. "Worthington Industries Acquire United Flat Rolled Products," *MetalPhonics* (June 1972), p. 1.
15. "A History of Worthington Industries," *The Open Door* (December 1986), p. 4.
16. Worthington Industries, Inc. 1972 Annual Report, p. 4.
17. Worthington Industries, Inc. 1974 Annual Report, p. 7.
18. "A History of Worthington Industries," *The Open Door* (December 1986), p. 4.
19. Worthington Industries, Inc. 1974 Annual Report, p. 6.
20. Worthington Industries, Inc. 1972 Annual Report, p. 4.
21. "Worthington Steel Constructs New Louisville Plant Addition," *MetalPhonics* (April 1973), p. 1.
22. Worthington Industries, Inc. 1973 Annual Report, p. 4.
23. Ralph Roberts, interviewed by the author, October 23, 1998. Transcript, pp. 5-6.

24. "A History of Worthington Industries," *The Open Door* (December 1986), p. 4.
25. Worthington Industries, Inc. 1974 Annual Report, p. 6.
26. "Armstrong Elected President of Worthington Industries," *MetalPhonics* (February 1974), p. 1.
27. Ibid.
28. Jack Graf, interviewed by David Patten, September 15, 1999. Transcript, p. 8.
29. Edward Ferkany, interviewed by the author, October 23, 1998. Transcript, p. 5.
30. Jack Marsh, interviewed by the author, April 14, 1999. Transcript, p. 5.
31. Ike Kelley, interviewed by the author, April 14, 1999. Transcript, p. 7.
32. Worthington Industries, Inc. 1974 Annual Report, p. 5.
33. Ibid.
34. Worthington Industries, Inc. 1974 Annual Report, p. 6.
35. Ibid.
36. Worthington Industries, Inc. 1975 Annual Report, p. 1.
37. Worthington Industries, Inc. 1974 Annual Report, pp. 1-2.
38. Ibid., p. 6.
39. Hall, p. 52.
40. Ibid., p. 62.
41. William Baldwin, "Spreading the Wealth." *Forbes* (April 27, 1981), p. 116.
42. Ibid.
43. Worthington Industries, Inc., 1975 Annual Report, p. 8.
44. Ibid., p. 5.
45. Ibid., p. 8.
46. Carol J. Loomis, "Corporate Stars that Brightened a Dark Decade," *Fortune* (April 30, 1984), pp. 24-32.
47. Bruce Ruhl, interviewed by David Patten, August 6, 1999. Transcript, p. 20.
48. "A History of Worthington Industries," *The Open Door* (December 1986), p. 4.

49. Jeff Phillips, "The Son Also Rises," *Columbus CEO* (April 1995), p. 2.
50. Ibid., p. 3.
51. Ibid.
52. Ibid.
53. Ibid.
54. Ibid.
55. Worthington Industries, Inc., 1976 Annual Report, p. 11.
56. "A History of Worthington Industries," *The Open Door* (December 1986), p. 4.
57. Worthington Industries, Inc., 1975 Annual Report, p. 5.
58. Ibid.
59. Worthington Industries, Inc., 1976 Annual Report, p. 11.
60. "A History of Worthington Industries," *The Open Door* (December 1986), p. 4.
61. Worthington Industries, Inc., 1977 Annual Report, p. 11.
62. "A History of Worthington Industries," *The Open Door* (December 1986), p. 4.
63. Harold "Butch" Dell, interviewed by David Patten, September 21, 1999. Transcript, p. 3.
64. Worthington Industries, Inc., 1977 Annual Report, p. 3.
65. Ibid., p. 5.
66. Ibid., p. 3.

Chapter Five

1. John Christie, interviewed by the author, April 15, 1999. Transcript, p. 10.
2. Eileen Alt Powell, "Factory Output Weakest since the 1974 Recession," *Boston Globe* (January 17, 1980). NewsLibrary.com reprint. (http://www.newslibrary.com)
3. Ibid.
4. *Boston Globe* (January 27, 1980). NewsLibrary.com
5. Ibid.
6. "Auto Layoffs Hit 190,925," *Boston Globe* (January 4, 1980). NewsLibrary.com reprint. (http://www.newslibrary.com)

7. Ibid.
8. Christopher Hall, *Steel Phoenix: The Fall and Rise of the U.S. Steel Industry* (New York: St. Martin's, 1997), p. 128.
9. Hall, p. 72.
10. Ibid.
11. Ibid.
12. Andrew Blum, "Steel Forges," *Philadelphia Daily News* (January 22 1980), p. B-15.
13. Hall, p. 129.
14. Donald Barnett and Robert Crandall, *Up from the Ashes: The Rise of the Steel Minimill in the United States* (Washington, D.C.: The Brookings Institution, 1986), p. 19.
15. Ibid.
16. Ibid.
17. Carol J. Loomis, "Corporate Stars that Brightened a Dark Decade," *Fortune* (April 30, 1984), pp. 224-232.
18. William Baldwin, "Spreading the Wealth," *Forbes* (April 27, 1981), p. 116.
19. Worthington Industries, Inc., 1980 Annual Report, p. 2.
20. Loomis, p. 224.
21. Jaclyn Fierman, "How to Make Money in Mature Markets," *Fortune* (November 25, 1985), p. 47.
22. Ibid.
23. Worthington Industries, Inc., 1980 Annual Report, p. 17.
24. Ibid., p. 5.
25. "A History of Worthington Industries 1955-1986," *The Open Door* (December 1986), p. 2.
26. "ACT Experiences Rapid Growth," *The Open Door* (April 1982), p. 2.
27. Ibid.
28. Ibid.
29. Worthington Industries, Inc., 1980 Annual Report, p. 7.
30. *Guardian Architectural Glass*, Printed by Guardian Industries (1984), p. 1.

31. "A History of Worthington Industries 1955-1986," *The Open Door* (December 1986), p. 2.
32. "U-Brand Corporation Founded 64 Years Ago," *The Open Door* (June 1982), p. 3.
33. Worthington Industries, Inc., 1980 Annual Report, p. 5.
34. "A History of Worthington Industries 1955-1986," *The Open Door* (December 1986), p. 2.
35. "Capital Die Tool and Machine," *The Open Door* (October 1987), p. 2.
36. Ibid.
37. "A History of Worthington Industries 1955-1986," *The Open Door* (December 1986), p. 2.
38. Ibid.
39. "Around the Company," *The Open Door* (fall 1989), p. 2.
40. "Presidential Visit," *The Open Door* (winter 1988), p. 1.
41. Bruce Ruhl, interviewed by David Patten, August 6, 1999. Transcript, p. 2.
42. Ike Kelley, interviewed by the author, April 14, 1999. Transcript, p. 11.
43. Worthington Industries, Inc., 1980 Annual Report, p. 7.
44. Ibid.
45. Worthington Industries, Inc., 1981 Annual Report, p. 2.
46. Ibid.
47. Edward Ferkany, interviewed by the author, October 23, 1998. Transcript, p. 4.
48. Worthington Industries, Inc., 1981 Annual Report, p. 2.
49. Ibid.
50. Robert Borel, interviewed by the author, April 15, 1999. Transcript, p. 6.
51. "A History of Worthington Industries 1955-1986," *The Open Door* (December 1986), p. 2.
52. Worthington Industries, Inc., 1981 Annual Report, p. 1.
53. Ibid.

54. John Hoerr, *And the Wolf Finally Came: The Decline of the American Steel Industry* (Pittsburgh: University of Pittsburgh Press, 1988), p. 106.
55. Hall, p. 73.
56. Roger Ahlbrandt, Richard Fruehan and Frank Giarratani, *The Renaissance of American Steel* (New York: Oxford University Press, 1996), p. 18.
57. Ahlbrandt, et al., p. 18.
58. Hall, p. 73.
59. Richard Preston, *American Steel: Hot Metal Men and the Resurrection of the Rust Belt* (New York: Prentice Hall Press, 1991), p. 80.
60. Irwin Ross, "A Paradise for Stock Pickers," *Fortune* (July 7, 1986), p. 80.
61. Ibid.
62. Ibid.
63. Ibid., p. 82.
64. Worthington Industries, Inc., 1982 Annual Report, p. 4.
65. Dale Brinkman, interviewed by David Patten, August 6, 1999. Transcript, p. 6.
66. Katie Byard, "U.S. Skimp-On-Quality Attitude Angers Author," *Akron Beacon Journal* (March 6, 1986), p. C-9.
67. Ibid.
68. Tom Peters, "Role Model in Steel," *U.S. News & World Report* (January 20, 1986), p. 100:2.
69. Jaclyn Fierman, "How to Make Money in Mature Markets," *Fortune* (November 25, 1985), p. 53.
70. Jack Marsh, interviewed by the author, April 14, 1999. Transcript, pp. 6-7.
71. Baldwin, p. 118.
72. Ibid.
73. Ibid.
74. Worthington Industries, Inc., 1983 Annual Report, p. 1.
75. Ibid., p. 10.
76. Carol J. Loomis, "Corporate Stars that Brightened a Dark

Decade," *Fortune* (April 30, 1984), p. 224.
77. Ibid.
78. Ibid.
79. Ibid.
80. Ibid.

Chapter Six

1. Ed Ferkany, interviewed by the author, October 23, 1998. Transcript, p. 3.
2. "January Production Up 1.1%," *Detroit Free Press* (February 16, 1984), p. 5C.
3. James Russell, "Economic Predictions Keyed to Election Year," *Detroit Free Press* (January 1, 1984), p. 6E.
4. Marcia Stepanek, "Strong '83 Auto Figures," *Detroit Free Press* (January 6, 1984), p. 9A.
5. James Russell, "Economic Predictions Keyed to Election Year," *Detroit Free Press* (January 1, 1984), p. 6E.
6. Roger Ahlbrandt, Richard Fruehan and Frank Giarratani. *The Renaissance of American Steel* (New York: Oxford University Press, 1996), pp. 16-17.
7. "Metals," *Forbes* (January 14, 1985), p. 170.
8. Ibid.
9. Ibid.
10. Ibid.
11. Ibid.
12. Ibid.
13. Ibid.
14. Worthington Industries, Inc., 1984 Annual Report, p. 2.
15. Ibid
16. David Hoag, interviewed by David Patten, September 22, 1999. Transcript, p. 4.
17. *The Open Door* (December 1985), p. 1.
18. Don Malenick, interviewed by the author, October 23, 1998. Transcript, p. 8.
19. Worthington Industries 1985 Annual Report, p. 5.
20. Ibid

21. Worthington Industries, Inc., 1984 Annual Report, p. 2.
22. Ibid., p. 1.
23. Ibid., p. 2.
24. Ibid.
25. Worthington Industries Inc., 1985 Annual Report, p. 6.
26. Ibid.
27. Ibid.
28. Ibid., p. 7.
29. Worthington Industries 1987 Annual Report, p. 4.
30. Worthington Industries 1984 Annual Report, p. 2.
31. Don Malenick, interviewed by the author, October 23, 1998. Transcript, p. 9.
32. John H. McConnell, interviewed by the author, October 23, 1998. Transcript, p. 52.
33. Worthington Industries 1987 Annual Report, p. 3.
34. Harold "Butch" Dell, interviewed by David Patten, September 21, 1999. Transcript, p. 5.
35. Carol J. Loomis, "Corporate Stars that Brightened a Dark Decade," *Forbes* (April 30, 1984), p. 231.
36. "A History of Worthington Industries 1955-1986," *The Open Door* (December 1986), p. 2.
37. "National Rolling Mills," *The Open Door* (August 1985), p. 2.
38. Ibid.
39. Ralph Roberts, interviewed by the author, October 23, 1998. Transcript, pp. 18-19.
40. Ibid.
41. Bruce Ruhl, interviewed by David Patten, August 6, 1999. Transcript, pp. 7-8.
42. "A History of Worthington Industries 1955-1986," *The Open Door* (December 1986), p. 2.
43. "Metals," *Forbes* (January 13, 1986), p. 176.
44. Worthington Industries 1987 Annual Report, p. 11.
45. "A History of Worthington Industries 1955-1986," *The*

Open Door (December 1986), p. 2.
46. Worthington Industries 1986 Annual Report, p. 8.
47. Ibid., p. 20.
48. Worthington Industries 1984 Annual Report , p. 3.
49. Ibid., p. 5.
50. "A History of Worthington Industries 1955-1986," *The Open Door* (December 1986), p. 2.
51. John Cummings, interviewed by Jon VanZile, September 10, 1999. Transcript, p. 10.
52. "Introducing Newman-Crosby Steel Inc.," *The Open Door* (June 1986), p. 2.
53. Ibid.
54. Ibid.
55. Ibid.
56. "President's Message," *The Open Door* (fall 1989), p. 1.
57. "A History of Worthington Industries 1955-1986," *The Open Door* (December 1986), p. 2.
58. "Introducing: Worthington Industries, Midland, Georgia," *The Open Door* (September 1986), p. 2.
59. Worthington Industries 1986 Annual Report, p. 4.
60. "Jackson Will Get Sheet Steel Center," *Detroit Free Press* (January 7, 1986), p. 4C.
61. Worthington Industries 1986 Annual Report, p. 6.
62. Paul Hocter, interviewed by Jon VanZile, September 23, 1999. Transcript, p. 5
63. "Jackson Steel Plant Dedicated," *Detroit Free Press* (June 16, 1987), p. 4B.
64. "Worthington Specialty Processing," *The Open Door* (June 1987), p. 1.
65. Ibid.
66. "New Team Members," *The Open Door* (March 1986), p. 1.
67. Christopher Hall, *Steel Phoenix: The Fall and Rise of the U.S. Steel Industry* (New York: St. Martin's Press, 1997), p. xiv.

68. "Chairman's Letter," *The Open Door* (March 1987), p. 1.

Chapter Six Sidebar: McConnell's Fountain

1. Alan Johnson, "Employees Honor McConnell with Floating Fountain," *The Columbus Dispatch* (July 4, 1986), Metro 1.
2. Ibid.

Chapter Seven

1. Worthington Industries 1988 Annual Report, p. 2.
2. Worthington Industries 1987 Annual Report, p. 2.
3. Ibid.
4. Ibid., p. 3.
5. Ibid., p. 2.
6. John Lear, "Steel on a Roll," *Detroit Free Press* (September 5, 1988), p. 1C.
7. Christopher Hall, *Steel Phoenix: The Fall and Rise of the U.S. Steel Industry* (New York: St. Martin's Press, 1997), p. 136.
8. Roger Ahlbrandt, Richard Fruehan and Frank Giarratani, *The Renaissance of American Steel* (New York: Oxford University Press, 1996), p. 18.
9. Worthington Industries 1988 Annual Report, p. 10.
10. Worthington Industries 1987 Annual Report, p. 20.
11. Ibid.
12. Ibid.
13. Ibid.
14. Worthington Industries 1988 Annual Report, p. 10.
15. Worthington Industries 1987 Annual Report. p. 20.
16. Robert Borel, interviewed by the author, April 15, 1999. Transcript, p. 16.
17. Harriet Monticello, "MSU Honors Three Business Alums," *Detroit Free Press* (April 1, 1987), p. 8B.

18. "A Message for the Future," *The Open Door* (summer 1988), p. 1.
19. Ibid.
20. Worthington Industries 1988 Annual Report, p. 1.
21. "Worthington Scores Big Gains for Year," *The Columbus Dispatch* (June 15, 1988), p. D2.
22. Worthington Industries 1988 Annual Report, p. 10.
23. Ibid.
24. "WC Canada," *The Open Door* (winter 1988), p. 2.
25. "Worthington Cylinder Goes Canadian," *The Open Door* (summer 1988), p. 1.
26. Ron Lietzke, "Worthington Industries' Stock Jumps," *The Columbus Dispatch* (July 15, 1988), p. 1E.
27. Ibid.
28. Robert Reiss and Sarah Mills Bacha, "Worthington Industries To Help Build Plant," *The Columbus Dispatch* (July 22, 1988), p. 1E.
29. Ibid.
30. Ron Lietzke, "Man of Steel McConnell Melds Metal with Mettle," *The Columbus Dispatch* (December 10, 1989), p. 1D.
31. John Lear, "Steel on a Roll," *Detroit Free Press* (September 5, 1988), p. 1C.
32. Ibid.
33. Ibid.
34. Ibid.
35. Ibid.
36. Ahlbrandt, et al., p. 6.
37. Hall, p. 65.
38. John Lear, "Steel on a Roll," *Detroit Free Press* (September 5, 1988), p. 1C.
39. Ibid.
40. Ahlbrandt, et al., p. 55.
41. Ibid.
42. Worthington Industries 1988 Annual Report, p. 5.
43. Ahlbrandt, et al., p. 18.
44. David Kirkpatrick, "Look Out, World, Here We Come," *Fortune* (June 20, 1988), p. 54.

45. Ibid.
46. Ibid.
47. "Presidential Visit," *The Open Door* (winter 1988), p. 1.
48. Ibid.
49. Ahlbrandt, et al., p. 18.
50. Don Malenick, interviewed by the author, October 23, 1998. Transcript, p. 7.
51. Barnet D. Wolf, "Company Nears Billion Dollar Mark," *The Columbus Dispatch* (September 16, 1988), p. 1B.
52. Ibid.
53. Ibid.
54. Worthington Industries 1989 Annual Report, p. 4.
55. Scott Robertson, "Toll-Processing Steel for End-Users' Needs," *Iron Age New Steel* (November 1994), p. 42.
56. Ibid.
57. "Georgia Plastics Plant Acquired," *Columbus Dispatch* (April 20, 1989), p. 1C.
58. Ibid.
59. John Lippert, "USW Says Ford Near Sale of Rouge Steel to Ohio Firm," *Detroit Free Press* (May 3, 1989), p. 1A.
60. Ibid.
61. Ibid.
62. Ibid.
63. Ibid.
64. Don Malenick, "President's Message," *The Open Door* (Fall 1989), p. 1.
65. Ibid.
66. Ibid.
67. Ibid.
68. Ron Lietzke, "Man of Steel McConnell Melds Metal with Mettle," *The Columbus Dispatch* (December 10, 1989), p. 1D.
69. Ibid.
70. Harold "Red" Poling, interviewed by the author, September 28, 1999. Transcript, p. 2.
71. Greg Gardner, "Ford Completes Sale of Rouge Steel," *Detroit Free Press* (December 16, 1989), p. 11A.

72. Barnet D. Wolf, "Steelmaker Gets New Investor," *Columbus Dispatch* (December 20, 1989), p. 1G.
73. Greg Gardner, "Ford Completes Sale of Rouge Steel," *Detroit Free Press* (December 16, 1989), p. 11A.
74. Ibid.
75. Barnet D. Wolf, "Worthington Industries Hits $1 Billion," *Columbus Dispatch* (June 16, 1989), p. 1G.
76. Ron Lietzke, "Man of Steel McConnell Melds Metal with Mettle," *The Columbus Dispatch* (December 10, 1989), p. 1D.
77. Ibid.

Chapter Eight

1. John Christie, interviewed by the author, April 14, 1999. Transcript, p. 16.
2. "The Outlook for 1990 — Steel: Business as Usual," *Business Journal Publishing* (January 1990), p. 43.
3. John D. McClain, "Fed Forecasts Slow Growth in '90s," *Akron Beacon Journal* (January 25, 1990), p. D4.
4. James Russell, "Economic Reports Send Wall Street on Deep Slide," *Akron Beacon Journal* (January 13, 1990), p. A9.
5. Bob Lewis, "Auto Layoffs Boost Claims for State Aid," *Akron Beacon Journal* (January 20, 1990), p. A10.
6. Christopher Hall, *Steel Phoenix: The Fall and Rise of the U.S. Steel Industry* (New York: St. Martin's Press, 1997), p. 268.
7. Worthington Industries 1990 Annual Report, p. 1.
8. Ibid.
9. Ibid., p. 12.
10. Ibid., pp. 1,8.
11. Ibid., p. 12.
12. Ibid.
13. Ibid., p. 1.

14. Ibid.
15. Ibid., p. 3.
16. Ibid., p. 11.
17. "New Precision Metal Plant," *The Open Door* (spring 1990), p. 5.
18. Mark Stier, interviewed by the author, April 14, 1999. Transcript, pp. 8-9.
19. Ibid.
20. Ibid., p. 9.
21. "Plant Drawn to Heart of Steel: Worthington Operation to Process, Pickle Metal," *Gary Post Tribune* (October 22, 1990), p. C1.
22. Ibid.
23. Ibid.
24. Mark Stier, interviewed by the author, April 14, 1999. Transcript, p. 9.
25. George J. McManus, "Processors Take on Pickling and Cold-Reducing, Too." *Iron Age New Steel* (March 1994), p. 18.
26. "Plant Drawn to Heart of Steel: Worthington Operation to Process, Pickle Metal," *Gary Post Tribune* (October 22, 1990), p. C1.
27. Jack Graf, interviewed by David Patten, September 15, 1999. Transcript, p. 4.
28. Mark Stier, interviewed by the author, April 14, 1999. Transcript, p. 10.
29. Worthington Industries 1992 Annual Report, p. 7.
30. Mark Stier, interviewed by the author, April 14, 1999. Transcript, p. 11.
31. "Plant Drawn to Heart of Steel: Worthington Operation to Process, Pickle Metal." *Gary Post Tribune* (October 22, 1990), p. C1.
32. Isidore, Chris. "Worthington Steel Slapped with Fine." *Gary Post-Tribune* (September 7, 1991), p. A1.
33. Ibid.
34. Ibid.
35. "Portage's Pickle Line Waste Treatment Facility Becomes

the Model for the U.S. EPA." *The Open Door* (August 1993), p. 4.
36. Ibid.
37. George J. McManus, "Processors Take on Pickling and Cold-Reducing, Too," *Iron Age New Steel* (March 1994), p. 18.
38. Ibid.
39. Ibid.
40. Barnet D. Wolf, "Worthington Welds Pact with Thyssen," *Columbus Dispatch* (July 13, 1990), p. 2E.
41. Worthington Industries 1992 Annual Report, p. 5.
42. Barnet D. Wolf, "Worthington Welds Pact with Thyssen," *Columbus Dispatch* (July 13, 1990), p. 2E.
43. Rick Ratliff, "Welding Plant Set for Detroit Venture will Test Laser Techniques," *Detroit Free Press* (July 12, 1990), p. 1E.
44. Worthington Industries 1993 Annual Report, p. 7.
45. Barnet D. Wolf, "Worthington Welds Pact with Thyssen," *Columbus Dispatch* (July 13, 1990), p. 2E.
46. Stanley L. Ream, "Mash and Laser Tailored Blank Welding," *Industrial Laser Review* (May 1995).
47. Ibid.
48. Ibid.
49. Worthington Industries 1991 Annual Report, p. 10.
50. Ibid., p. 11.
51. Barnet D. Wolf, "Looking for Record Year," *Columbus Dispatch* (September 20, 1991), p. 1F.
52. Ibid.
53. Worthington Industries 1992 Annual Report, p. 9.
54. "Cylinder Maker Purchases Firm," *Columbus Dispatch* (January 28, 1992), p. 2D.
55. Ibid.
56. *The Open Door* (November 1993), p. 1.
57. Ibid., p. 3.

58. Ibid., p. 2.
59. John Christie, interviewed by the author, April 14, 1999. Transcript, p. 15.
60. Ralph Roberts, interviewed by the author, April 14, 1999. Transcript, p. 20.
61. Peter Binzen, "Worthington-Armstrong Alliance is a Formidable 1-2 Punch," *Philadelphia Inquirer* (November 25, 1996), p. C3.
62. Ralph Roberts, interviewed by the author, April 14, 1999. Transcript, p. 22.
63. Worthington Industries 1992 Annual Report, p. 9.
64. Ralph Roberts, interviewed by the author, April 14, 1999. Transcript, p. 20.
65. Peter Binzen, "Worthington-Armstrong Alliance is a Formidable 1-2 Punch," *Philadelphia Inquirer* (November 25, 1996), p. C3.
66. Ibid.
67. "Earnings Higher at Worthington," *Columbus Dispatch* (March 13, 1992), p. 2E.
68. Worthington Industries 1992 Annual Report, p. 2.
69. Ibid., p. 3.
70. Ibid.
71. Pete Klisares, interviewed by David Patten, August 6, 1999. Transcript, p. 2.

Chapter Nine

1. *The Open Door* (April 1993), p. 4.
2. Worthington Industries 1993 Annual Report, p. 2.
3. Barnet D. Wolf, "Area Firms among Best Places to Work," *Columbus Dispatch* (January 23, 1993), p. 1-D.
4. Ibid.
5. Ibid.
6. Ibid.
7. Barnet D. Wolf, "Son to Replace Founding Father of Worthington Industries," *Columbus Dispatch* (March 10, 1993), p. 1-G.

8. Ibid.
9. Ibid.
10. Ibid.
11. Jeff Phillips, "The Son Also Rises," *Columbus CEO* (April 1995), p. 4.
12. Ibid.
13. Ibid.
14. Ibid.
15. Ibid.
16. Barnet D. Wolf, "Son to Replace Founding Father of Worthington Industries," *Columbus Dispatch* (March 10, 1993), p. 1-G.
17. *The Open Door* (April 1993), p. 4.
18. Worthington Industries 1993 Annual Report, p. 2.
19. Phil Porter, "Focus on Quality: More Companies Adopt TQM to Enhance Competitiveness," *Columbus Dispatch* (April 18, 1993), p. 1-G.
20. Ibid.
21. Jeff Phillips, "The Son Also Rises," *Columbus CEO* (April 1995), p. 5.
22. Phil Porter, "Focus on Quality: More Companies Adopt TQM to Enhance Competitiveness," *Columbus Dispatch* (April 18, 1993), p. 1-G.
23. Ibid.
24. Ibid.
25. Ibid.
26. Ibid.
27. "Worthington Industries Reports Record Results for Quarter, Year," *Columbus Dispatch* (June 15, 1994), p. 1-H.
28. Ibid.
29. Ron Lietzke, "Worthington Plans French Plant," *Columbus Dispatch* (September 17, 1993), p. 1-B.
30. Worthington Industries 1994 Annual Report, p. 3.
31. "Worthington Industries Building Plastics Plant," *Columbus Dispatch* (March 26, 1993), p. 2-F.

32. Worthington Industries 1995 Annual Report, p. 3.
33. Ibid., p. 14.
34. Peter Binzen, "Worthington-Armstrong Alliance is a Formidable 1-2-3 Punch," *Philadelphia Inquirer* (November 25, 1996), p. C-3.
35. "Worthington Industries Signs Mexican Venture," *Columbus Dispatch* (September 30, 1994), p. 1-D.
36. "Worthington Industries Looks at Mexico," *The Open Door* (December 1992), p. 4.
37. Ibid.
38. Ibid.
39. "Worthington Industries Signs Mexican Venture," *Columbus Dispatch* (September 30, 1994), p. 1-D.
40. Dennis Blackford, "Worthington Industries Focuses on Keeping its Workers Healthy," *Columbus Dispatch* (June 9, 1994), p. 1-F.
41. Ibid.
42. James Mason, interviewed by the author and David Patten, April 14, 1998. Transcript, pp. 2-3.
43. Ibid.
44. Ibid.
45. Dennis Blackford, "Worthington Industries Focuses on Keeping its Workers Healthy," *Columbus Dispatch* (June 9, 1994), p. 1-F.
46. James Mason, interviewed by the author and David Patten, April 14, 1998. Transcript, pp. 9-10.
47. Laurie Loscocco, "McConnell Backs Center," *Columbus Dispatch* (November 15, 1994), p. 1-A.
48. Ibid.
49. Worthington Industries 1995 Annual Report, p. 16-17.
50. Ron Carter, "Worthington Gets Boost from Plant,"

Columbus Dispatch (November 24, 1995), p. 1-D.
51. Ibid.
52. Ibid.
53. Ibid.
54. "Worthington Machine Technology," *The Open Door* (December 1995), p. 2.
55. Ibid.
56. Ibid.
57. "Managing Information Increases Worthington Industries' Productivity," *The Open Door* (May 1994), p. 3.
58. "Local Firm Wins Ranking in Magazine," *Columbus Dispatch* (October 16, 1995), p. 2.
59. Worthington Industries 1995 Annual Report, p. 2.
60. Ron Carter, "Worthington Plans Steel Mill, Plant," *Columbus Dispatch* (September 23, 1994), p. 1-E.
61. "To Succeed, Steelmakers Must Maintain Competitive Edge," *Metal/Center News* (July 1995), p. 86.
62. Ron Carter, "Worthington Plans Steel Mill, Plant," *Columbus Dispatch* (September 23, 1994), p. 1-E.
63. Ibid.
64. John F. Geer, Jr., "Cyclical Lite," *Financial World* (March 25, 1996), p. 44.
65. Ron Carter, "Worthington Industries is Mum on Mill," *Columbus Dispatch* (November 4, 1994), p. 2-B.
66. Ibid.
67. Ibid.
68. John F. Geer, Jr., "Cyclical Lite," *Financial World* (March 25, 1996), p. 44.
69. Ron Carter, "Worthington Halts Plans for Minimill," *Columbus Dispatch* (May 10, 1995), p. 1-G.
70. Ibid.
71. Ibid.
72. "To Succeed, Steelmakers Must Maintain Competitive Edge," *Metal/Center News* (July 1995), p. 86.

73. John F. Geer, Jr., "Cyclical Lite," *Financial World* (March 25, 1996), p. 44.
74. Internal company memo dated August 20, 1995. Worthington Archive.
75. Worthington Industries 1995 Annual Report, p. 2.
76. Don Malenick, "President's Message," *The Open Door* (December 1995), p. 1.
77. Ibid.
78. Worthington Industries 1995 Annual Report, p. 5.
79. Ibid.
80. Ibid.

Chapter Ten

1. Worthington Industries 1996 Annual Report, p. 3.
2. Ibid.
3. John F. Geer, "Cyclical Lite." *Financial World* (March 25, 1996), p. 3.
4. Worthington Industries 1996 Annual Report pp. 4, 19.
5. Ron Carter, "Steel Processor Looking Forward to Growth Years," *Columbus Dispatch* (September 22, 1995), p. 1-B.
6. John F. Geer, "Cyclical Lite." *Financial World* (March 25, 1996), p. 3.
7. Ibid.
8. Howard Rudnitsky, "Pumping Steel," *Forbes* (January 1, 1996), p. 154.
9. Worthington Industries 1998 Annual Report, p. 17.
10. John P. McConnell, interviewed by the author, October 23, 1998. Transcript, p. 15.
11. Ron Carter, "Worthington Kicks Off Expansion Mode," *Columbus Dispatch* (January 17, 1996), p. 1-B.
12. Ibid.
13. John F. Geer, "Cyclical Lite." *Financial World* (March 25, 1996), p. 3.
14. "Steel: The Innovative Choice in Residential Markets." Web site of The American Iron

and Steel Institute. http://www.steel.org/facts/innovative.htm
15. Ron Carter, "Worthington Kicks Off Expansion Mode," *Columbus Dispatch* (January 17, 1996), p. 1-B.
16. Ed Ponko, interviewed by David Patten, September 9, 1999. Transcript, p. 5
17. John P. McConnell, interviewed by the author, October 23, 1998. Transcript, p. 16.
18. Ed Ponko, interviewed by David Patten, September 9, 1999. Transcript, p. 8.
19. Ron Carter, "Worthington Kicks Off Expansion Mode," *Columbus Dispatch* (January 17, 1996), p. 1-B.
20. Ibid.
21. Dennis Blackford, "Worthington Buys Canadian Cylinder Maker," *Columbus Dispatch* (June 29,1996), p. 1-H.
22. Ibid.
23. Ibid.
24. Worthington Industries 1997 Annual Report, pp. 4, 11.
25. Stephen Senkowski, interviewed by Jon VanZile, September 24, 1999. Transcript, p. 14.
26. Worthington Industries 1996 Annual Report, p. 5.
27. Ron Carter, "Business Trailblazer McConnell Steps Down," *Columbus Dispatch* (September 20, 1996), p. 1-A.
28. Ron Carter, "Man of Steel: Outgoing Chairman John H. McConnell Talks about His Life Work, Forging the Successful Worthington Industries," *Columbus Dispatch* (September 29, 1996), p. 1-F.
29. Ibid.
30. Ibid.
31. Steve Wright, "McConnell Joins Columbus Hall of Fame," *Columbus Dispatch* (October 10, 1998), p. 1-B.

32. Ibid.
33. Pete Klisares, interviewed by David Patten, August 6, 1999. Transcript, pp. 4-5.
34. "McConnell Gets Gridiron Award," *Columbus Dispatch* (December 9, 1998), p. 1-B.
35. Ibid.
36. Worthington Industries 1997 Annual Report, p. 10.
37. Ron Carter, "Worthington Forges Deal," *Columbus Dispatch* (February 4, 1997), p. 1-D.
38. Worthington Industries 1997 Annual Report, p. 8.
39. Ron Carter, "Worthington Forges Deal," *Columbus Dispatch* (February 4, 1997), p. 1-D.
40. Ken Vagnini, interviewed by David Patten, September 9, 1999. Transcript, p. 6.
41. Ron Carter, "Worthington Forges Deal," *Columbus Dispatch* (February 4, 1997), p. 1-D.
42. "The Gerstenslager Story," Company publication, inside flap.
43. Ibid.
44. John Christie, interviewed by the author, April 15, 1999. Transcript, pp. 5-6.
45. Ibid.
46. Worthington Industries 1998 Annual Report, p. 9.
47. Worthington Industries 1997 Annual Report, p. 9.
48. Worthington Industries 1998 Annual Report, p. 9.
49. Harold "Butch" Dell, interviewed by David Patten, September 21, 1999. Transcript, p. 11.
50. Worthington Industries 1998 Annual Report, p. 9.
51. James Ballard, interviewed by David Patten, September 21, 1999. Transcript, pp. 3-4.
52. Ibid., p. 7.
53. Mary Wood-Anderson, interviewed by Lisa Allen, May 1999.

54. James Ballard, interviewed by David Patten, September 21, 1999. Transcript, p. 9.
55. Jack Graf, interviewed by David Patten, September 15, 1999. Transcript, p. 12.
56. James Ballard, interviewed by David Patten, September 21, 1999. Transcript, pp. 11-12.
57. Worthington Industries 1998 Annual Report, p. 5.
58. James Ballard, interviewed by David Patten, September 21, 1999. Transcript, p. 14.
59. Robert Levering and Milton Moskowitz, "The 100 Best Companies to Work for in America," *Fortune* (January 12, 1998).
60. Ibid.
61. Ibid.
62. Ron Carter, "Worthington Industries Puts Big Spin on Europe," *Columbus Dispatch* (February 24, 1998), p. 1-D.
63. Jeffrey Sheban, "Steelmaker Buys Stake in Brazilian Plant," *Columbus Dispatch* (February 12, 1997), p. 1-F.
64. Ibid.
65. Ron Carter, "Worthington Industries Puts Big Spin on Europe," *Columbus Dispatch* (February 24, 1998), p. 1-D.
66. Ibid.
67. Ibid.
68. Worthington Industries press release, May 24, 1999.
69. Ibid.
70. Ibid.
71. Worthington Industries 1998 Summary Annual Report, p. 9.
72. Ibid.
73. Chris Adams, "Sale of Three Units of Worthington Is Under Study," *The Wall Street Journal* (April 2, 1998).
74. Ibid.
75. Ibid.
76. Ibid.
77. Ibid.
78. Ibid.
79. Ibid.

80. Worthington Industries 1998 Annual Report, p. 17.
81. Worthington Industries press release, June 18, 1998.
82. Worthington Industries press release, November 3, 1998.
83. Worthington Industries press release, February 10, 1999.
84. Ibid.
85. Worthington Industries press release, March 2, 1999.
86. Worthington Industries press release, May 27, 1999.
87. Worthington Industries press release, May 6, 1999.
88. "Transformation Kick-Off," Worthington Industries internal publication, June 1999.
89. Ibid.
90. Ibid.
91. John Christie, interviewed by the author, April 15, 1999. Transcript, p. 19.
92. Worthington Industries press release, March 2, 1999.
93. Dale Brinkman, interviewed by David Patten, August 6, 1999. Transcript, p. 7.
94. Worthington Industries press release, March 2, 1999.
95. John Christie, interviewed by the author, April 15, 1999. Transcript, pp. 1-2.
96. Cathy Mayne Lyttle, interview with the author, February 4, 2002. Transcript, p. 4.
97. Ken Vagnini, interviewed by the author, January 18, 2002. Transcript, p. 8.
98. Nick Anderson, "Bush Orders Steel Inquiry," *Los Angeles Times*, 6 June 2001, Part 3, Pg. 1
99. Ed Ferkany, interviewed by the author, December 14, 2001. Transcript, p. 5.
100. Ed Ferkany, interviewed by the author, December 14, 2001. Transcript, pp. 4-5.
101. John Lamprinakos, interviewed by the author, December 18, 2001. Transcript. p. 6.

102. "Worthington Industries Announces Management Changes," PR Newswire, 11 January 2001.

103. PR Newswire, 20 June 2002.

104. Ibid.

105. Mark Niquette, "Steel Maker's Outlook Brightens," *Columbus Dispatch*, 20 December 2001, p. 1D.

106. Mark Niquette, "Company to close six plants," *Columbus Dispatch*, 25 January 2002, p. 1B.

107. Robert Levering and Milton Moskowitz, "The 100 Best Companies to Work For," *Fortune*, 4 February 2001, p. 72.

108. "America's Most Admired Companies," *Fortune*, 4 March 2002.

109. Jon Birger, "The 30 Best Stocks," *Money*, January 2002.

110. Pat Cotter, interviewed by the author, January 25, 2002. Transcript, pp. 3-4.

111. Ibid

112. Ken Vagnini, interviewed by the author, January 18, 2002. Transcript, p. 8.

113. Ed Ponko, interviewed by the author, December 14, 2001. Transcript, pp. 4-5.

114. Jon Birger, "The 30 Best Stocks," *Money*, January 2002.

115. Ed Ponko, interviewed by the author, October 25, 2002. Transcript, p. 10.

116. Ibid.

117. Ibid.

118. John Christie, interviewed by the author, November 26, 2002. Transcript, p. 5.

119. John Christie, interviewed by the author, December 14, 2001. Transcript, p. 14.

120. John Baldwin, interviewed by David Patten, August 6, 1999. Transcript, p. 10.

121. Press release, 12 December 2002, Worthington Industries Archive.

122. Cathy Mayne Lyttle, interviewed by the author, February 4, 2002. Transcript, p. 13.

123. Barnet D. Wolf, "Mr. Mac bidding company farewell," *Columbus Dispatch*.

124. John P. McConnell, interviewed by the author, February 13, 2002. Transcript, p. 4.

125. Ibid.

INDEX